PRAISE FOR SPIRIT LED INSTEAD

"Are you looking for a direct and simple way to embrace your life with more joy, illuminate the love within you, and live from the wisest part of yourself? Spirit Led Instead is the treasured resource you'll find yourself returning to again and again. Read this book carefully, and these life-altering tools will allow you to consciously change your world."

- *Marci Shimoff, #1 New York Times bestselling author of* Love for No Reason *and* Happy for No Reason

"There is a lovely quality to this book; it is simple and wise, personal and at the same time expansive. You'll be guided through a clarifying process that will help you reshape your perceptual habits and life. Jenai Lane brings higher wisdom into many practical applications for transforming yourself and your world."

- *Penney Peirce, author of* Leap of Perception, Frequency, *and* The Intuitive Way

"This book is an amazing vehicle for the innovator who wants to lead by 'being the change for the world.' The reader who applies these clearly described, well-tested, practical tools for transformation will 'let Spirit lead' toward more joy, peace, fulfillment, purpose, creativity, and abundance in life."

- *Gundi Heinemann, author of* Orbs: Their Mission and Messages of Hope

"Jenai presents concepts and exercises that make it easy and fun for anyone to access their true spirit and live a purposeful life."

- *Debbie Gisonni, business leader and author of* The Goddess of Happiness *and* Vita's Will

"This book is the most practical, efficient, grace-filled approach to self-awareness and aligning to spirit that I have ever read."

- *Dr. Megan Scott, clinical psychologist and master yoga teacher*

PRAISE FROM CLIENTS

"What you most want in life and of life may be waiting on the other side."
- Mike Netzel

"This type of coaching is the fast track to Real Freedom!"
- Tim Wood

"A life-changing experience that is beyond your wildest imagination. It will provide you with tools for your life that operate from a much higher level of integrity and power."
- Sunil Patel

"How clear and concise your teachings are, mingled with an authentic feeling of love, compassion, and steadfastness…"
- Marie Glon

"I can honestly say that it is the best money I've ever spent on anything in my life—including my very expensive and 'prestigious' college education."
- Natalie Doel

"This coaching has largely impacted how I think and feel today. It has enhanced my love and respect for who I am."
- Rob Gispert

"You will learn so much about who you really are. You will learn to love yourself."
- Sherry Huffman

SPIRIT LED
INSTEAD

SPIRIT

MIND   BODY

The Little Tool Book of Limitless Transformation

Jenai Lane Creator of The Spirit Coach® Method

Spirit Led Instead
The Little Tool Book of Limitless Transformation
By Jenai Lane
Spirit Coach Press

Published by Spirit Coach Press, San Rafael, California
Copyright ©2013 by Jenai Lane

Developmental Editor: Stephanie Marohn, www.stephaniemarohn.com
Copyeditor: Patti McKenna, www.writeandedit.wordpress.com/about
Copyeditor: Audrey Mackaman, www.audreyedits.com
Proofreader: Pamela Thomas Elkins
Cover Design: Ronnie Sharpe and Zoe Lonergan
Graphic Art: John Otto
Interior Design: Ashley Hemmen
Author Photo: Lori A. Cheung, www.theportraitphotographer.com

Library of Congress Control Number: 2011962454
ISBN: 978-0-9849366-0-1

For Personal Use Only. No part of this book may be used for clinical, commercial, or professional use without licensed permission. To learn more about Spirit Coach® Training or becoming certified in the Spirit Coach® Method, please contact coach@spiritcoachtraining.com.

To order additional copies, please contact Spirit Coach Press.

Visit www.spiritcoachtraining.com to learn more about receiving one-on-one coaching in this transformational method.

This book is dedicated to all those who have the courage

to follow their spirit's path, one step at a time.

The greatest journey is the one we take within.

TABLE OF CONTENTS

INTRODUCTION: MY JOURNEY TO BECOMING SPIRIT LED INSTEAD 9

CHAPTER ONE: OUT OF YOUR MIND AND INTO YOUR SPIRIT 15

TRANSFORMATIONAL TOOL #1: QUIET YOUR MIND 23

TRANSFORMATIONAL TOOL #2: THE LET GO AND KNOW LIST 27

CHAPTER TWO: FIVE MINUTES TO FREEDOM AND FULFILLMENT 31

TRANSFORMATIONAL TOOL #3: CENTERING—YOUR GROUNDING CORD 42

TRANSFORMATIONAL TOOL #4: CLEARING—YOUR SPIRIT BUBBLE 44

TRANSFORMATIONAL TOOL #5: CONNECTING—YOUR CONNECTION TO SPIRIT 47

CHAPTER THREE: HOW TO DO LESS AND BE MORE WHILE DISCOVERING 53
THE REAL YOU

TRANSFORMATIONAL TOOL #6: SET A DAILY INTENTION 60

TRANSFORMATIONAL TOOL #7: CREATE "BE TIME" 64

CHAPTER FOUR: THE POWER OF INTEGRITY TO LEAD YOU TO YOUR 67
HIGHEST VISION

TRANSFORMATIONAL TOOL #8: HOW TO DISCOVER YOUR INTEGRITY 73
HOLES AND REPAIR THEM

Transformational Tool #9: Rose-Release Mediation   77

Transformational Tool #10: Replacing "I Should" with "I Choose"   81

Chapter Five: Change the Way You See the World and the   87
World Changes

Transformational Tool #11: Turn Energy Drains to Energy Givers   91

Transformational Tool #12: Forgive for Good   94

Transformational Tool #13: Gratitude List with a Twist   99

Transformational Tool #14: The Color of Your Spirit Bubble   105
(Change Your Vibration)

Chapter Six: How to Unleash the Visionary in You   109

Transformational Tool #15: Top 10 Things That Make Your   113
Heart Sing

Transformational Tool #16: Draw Your Vision   118

Transformational Tool #17: Journal Your Vision   119

Chapter Seven: Let What You Seek Find You   125

Transformational Tool #18: The Co-Creation To-Do List   127

Transformational Tool Checklist   132

Acknowledgments   141

About The Author   143

INTRODUCTION

My Journey to Becoming Spirit Led Instead

My fifteen minutes of fame lasted for a couple of years. I had what I had always thought I wanted: a wildly successful business, appearances on national TV, magazine articles written about me, woman entrepreneur of the year. My business success was my dream. Here I was living it, and yet I didn't feel fulfilled.

Of course, I never said this out loud—that would be ungrateful. I knew, though, that something was missing. It felt like a deep hole inside of me that was longing to be filled and everything I had thought would fill it did not. I was determined to find what would. I left my career, my home, and my life as I knew it and went on a spiritual pilgrimage of sorts. I was determined to find the answer to my questions: Who am I? Why am I here? What will truly bring me peace and deep fulfillment? How can I contribute? This led me to search around the world and back again.

In the course of my pilgrimage, I sat with a shaman in Bali, studied with a medicine man in California, and channeled healing energy with John of God in Brazil, among many other seeking experiences. Each time, I asked the spiritual teacher what I should do with my life and what my next business venture should be, desperately hoping one of them would tell me. Looking back, I bet this was comical to these enlightened masters. Each gave me a variation on the same answer: "Jenai, it is not about doing; just be." This infuriated me because I had no idea what they were talking about. I went from one teacher to another, attended countless seminars, and read piles of books on spirituality, hoping that the next teacher, workshop, or book would somehow change me. It's not that these things didn't help me—they did—but it was in the seeking that I was never really able to find my truth.

That is, until one day I was driving somewhere near Sedona, Arizona, trying to locate the retreat center where I thought I would finally find myself. It soon became clear that I was lost. How ironic—how could I find myself if I couldn't even find the place where that was supposed to happen? I became increasingly frustrated as I drove in circles, seemingly unable to get where I wanted to go. It was the perfect metaphor for my life. Out of desperation, I pulled over to ask for help. For some reason, I looked up, and there was a giant billboard right in front of me. In big black letters, it said: "If you can't find God, you moved." I had always been one for signs—and this was literally a sign, just in case I wasn't paying attention. It was clearly a message intended for me. I'll never forget the feeling of realizing I was only lost because I had become disconnected from my spirit, the Divine in me. I looked toward the heavens, cried, and then laughed. It appeared the joke was on me.

During all the time I'd spent running from one spiritual experience to the next, I had been looking for the answers outside myself, not aware that my truth could only come from within.

Shortly after this realization, I found myself at a school called the Foundation for Spiritual Development, a nonprofit organization dedicated to helping people understand themselves as spirit. I was able to bloom in this environment, first as a student and, subsequently, as a teacher. It was like a graduate school for my spirit. It was there that I really developed my intuition, the voice of spirit. This voice guided me to a deep understanding of who I am, why I am here, and the contribution I am here to make. It was a very different voice from the one I was used to. I discovered that the old voice came from my mind or ego identity. My mind was filled with so many voices that weren't my own: the voices of my teachers, my parents, my friends, my community, and my culture. The voice of my mind, influenced by all these other voices, could not possibly know what truth was for me, even though it claimed to. As I learned to apply tools to exit the vantage point of my mind, my spirit took the lead. This is what being spirit led is all about.

My spirit led me to the work I do today: coaching and teaching others to awaken their Divine potential. For more than a decade, I have been training business leaders to be spirit led through the Spirit Coach Method®, which I developed and which consists of a series of transformational tools. The method came to me from what I call Divine guidance. I have been receiving this Divine guidance since I became spirit led. Let me explain. Before a coaching session with a client, I sit down and meditate, asking how I can serve the best interests of my client. I am always in awe of the answers I receive from spirit, including specific information about the client's block and the tools that can help the client transcend it. Over the years, I have received hundreds of tools, which are universally applicable even though I received the tool for a particular client. I have used these tools with hundreds of people in my Spirit Coach Method seminars, retreats, and trainings. The method also includes some of the tools I learned, and still teach, at the Foundation for Spiritual Development. They have been changed, as guided by spirit, to serve a broader audience.

The Spirit Coach Method tools in this book are not about fixing something in you or changing the external, but are intended instead to focus on revealing the spirit within. They are tried and true. My clients and I are practical, and we want to see results from the tools we employ. Without tools, I have found that it can seem impossible to transform. Even with the best intentions, we may not know how to get from point A to point B on the spiritual path. Tools are the way that I know to get us there.

The transformational tools in this book will give you a way to live from your own spirit. This path is what I would call "Practical Spirituality." There is no dogma—only tools that anyone can use to improve his or her life. Because it is non-dogmatic, this process has nothing to do with a particular religion. Spirit is the essence of every human being. You might find spirituality in religion, but you won't find religion in spirituality. All paths, ultimately, lead to spirit. Whatever path you are on, though different for each of us, these tools can be used to enhance your life. The beauty of being spirit led is that you are able to determine what is true for you through your own experience of spirit. There is no longer a need for a priest, guru, teacher, or anyone outside of you in order for you to access your Divinity. Everything you have been searching for is within.

Today, all I have to do is look at my life and the people I serve and I can see the evidence of what a spirit-led life can do. I now have a career doing the work I truly love to do. I coach and teach others in the Spirit Coach Method and also certify those who are called to the path of being a Spirit Coach. I lead spiritual retreats in beautiful places with amazing people and also take groups on spiritual pilgrimages to see John of God in Brazil. At the Foundation for Spiritual Development, I teach healing, intuition development, and living from spirit. In addition, I help run a weekly center that offers free energetic healing to the public. I have the privilege of blessing babies, marrying people, and helping people cross over. All of these things and more are an extension of my spirit's path. If you had told me fifteen years ago that this is the life I would be living, I would have said you were out of your mind. As it happened, "out of my mind" was exactly where I needed to go to be spirit led.

The tools in this book can support you, too, in aligning with your spirit and discovering your best life. You can access whatever it is that eludes you at this moment—whether it is your purpose, your intuition, your creative genius, your vision, your power, or your fulfillment—by aligning with your spirit. That alignment is your birthright; it is who you are. In our culture, we are taught to ignore spirit and pay more attention to logic. As logic is mind-based, it can never lead you toward your true path because the mind is disconnected from who you are. Yes, the mind is a handy tool and we need it to function, but when the mind is driving, who you are—your spirit—takes a backseat and you never arrive at your destination—you.

The truth is that no one can tell you your truth. It has to come from within. The good news is that your truth is accessible to you once you connect to your spirit. It may be buried, but with the right tools, your spirit will emerge. When it does, you gain access to a part of you that is limitless. From here, nothing is impossible. When you are spirit led, what you're looking for is found, life unfolds at an aligned pace, and your manifested creations follow your true path. It is so simple. After a while, your spirit becomes the loud and predominant voice, no longer so easy to ignore. Then life becomes the one you were meant to live—yours.

What happens with the application of the simple Spirit Coach Method tools is best said by one of my clients. "The tools you have taught me to get in touch with my spirit continue to guide me along my path, and my current sense of self-worth, self-trust, and self-love is unmatched by anything I have ever felt in this lifetime. I feel I am stepping more and more onto my Divine path."

Blessings to be spirit led instead,

Jenai

CHAPTER ONE

Out of Your Mind and into Your Spirit

"To the mind that is still, the whole universe surrenders."
- Lao Tzu

I used to schedule my day in fifteen-minute increments. Have you ever run to the bathroom at the absolute last second just because you were so busy? Well, that is how my life was. I was a business leader building a growing consumer product company, which had more employees than I knew how to manage. We were listed in *Entrepreneur Magazine* as one of the top fastest-growing companies in America. I was twenty-eight years old and on my way to being burned out by thirty. The road paved with success was proving to be less fulfilling than I had imagined.

One day, I did something completely out of the norm, and it changed my life forever. On this particular day, I was feeling trapped and needed a break to just be alone. I remembered reading an article that said taking your focus off your routine, even for a short time, could get your creative juices flowing again. I was hoping for a little more than creativity—I wanted to feel free again. So I told my staff I would be gone for the next two hours, although I had no idea where or what I was going to be doing in those two hours. At the time, this seemed crazy, even to me. There was always something to do and never enough time to do it in, but this compulsion to escape for a while was strong enough to pull me out of the office.

I climbed in my car and began driving, even though I had no idea where I was going. This was even more ridiculous to me. My mind questioned my actions, asking, *Why am I wasting my time?* There was some other part of me, however, that was suddenly separate from my mind that said, *Keep driving.* So I did.

I listened to this small voice that seemed to be me, but I hadn't heard it for a very long time. It kept saying, *Drive this way, keep going.* I would stop on occasion and ask, "Are we there yet?" like a child on a long car trip, anxious to arrive at their destination. This has been symptomatic of my life, always wanting to get where I was going. Then, when I got there, I was not completely satisfied, so off again I would go to the next place.

I was driving through a neighborhood in San Francisco that I was completely unfamiliar with and saw a Starbucks on the corner. I heard, *Pull over.* You can imagine my relief. Starbucks was a place I could very much relate to and feel comfortable in. In fact, it kept me going through my sixty-hour work weeks.

I ordered my usual grande soy latte and sat down in a chair with a view of the street outside, enjoying some familiarity in this strange experiment I seemed to be participating in. After several minutes passed by, I noticed a homeless man walking across the street toward Starbucks. As I studied him, I realized I knew him. He was a man from the neighborhood I currently lived in; however, I hadn't seen him in at least two years. He looked very much the same as I remembered him, dressed in very elegant, preppy-tattered clothing, as if he came out of a J.Crew catalogue and never changed his clothes again.

I was elated to see him because I thought he had died. For many years, he had been a fixture in my neighborhood. I would often buy him coffee, and he would smile and mutter incoherently. There was something about him I could relate to, something that attracted me to him. He had something I wanted, which seemed absurd, considering he lived on the street and was mostly incomprehensible.

Without hesitating, I jumped out of my seat and ran out of Starbucks to greet him. "Remember me, remember me?" I shouted. "You hung out in my neighborhood. I am so happy to see you. How are you?"

Before I could finish, he turned and looked at me with a clarity and certainty so powerful, it was as if a wind came and blew right into my face and said, *Wake up, child.* Needless to say, I was paying attention. Staring deep into my eyes with a power beyond the physical, he said, "You want to help people, but you do not know how." Then he walked away.

It hit me like a ton of bricks. I could hardly breathe. There was a resonance there that was so deep, it made me stop in my tracks. In that moment, I knew there was some greater vision for my life that I had been willing to ignore. I was meant to help people, and he was right—I didn't know how. This encounter made me begin to ask those deeper questions of myself: Who am I? Why am I here? How can I contribute? This was the beginning of my path to being spirit led instead.

After this brief encounter, I knew my life needed to change, but I wasn't sure how to make that happen. Then, I had a dream that pointed me in the right direction. In the dream, I was in my version of hell, a meat locker with animal carcasses hanging from the ceiling that were somehow blocking my path; I couldn't get out. Until I found a doorway. On the other side was a woman who was motioning to me to follow her toward what looked like a gourmet food festival perched on top of rolling green hills; it was my version of heaven. I had never seen this woman before she appeared in my dream. A few days later, I was at a women's business luncheon, and the very same woman from my dream was sitting at the table where I was eating lunch. I knew spirit was nudging me to talk to her. This was another sign I couldn't ignore.

I went over to her, and she began to tell me about a spiritual retreat she was attending and asked if I wanted to go. I never heard the word *yes* so quickly jump out of my mouth. The wise part of me knew this was where I might find some answers to the mounting questions that were unanswered.

A few weeks later, I found myself in Maui at a week-long spiritual retreat, but it felt more like spiritual boot camp. We were isolated in the middle of the jungle. There was no phone, no Internet, and no outside communication of any kind. You get the picture. I was beside myself. It was the first time I was unable to communicate with my staff, my friends, and my family. This was really stretching my comfort zone.

In fact, the entire experience forced me out of my box. The first few days, I kept thinking, *What am I doing here? Who are these weird people I am with? Why did I listen to spirit, anyway?* Over the course of that week, we meditated, we prayed, and we went within for guidance. Things got progressively better as the days went by. For the first time, I found myself beginning to let go of the false picture I had painted of myself as a successful, hard-hitting businesswoman. It was like a crack in the facade opened me up and my own light started shining through. This light had nothing to do with the ego identity I thought I was; in fact, it made me begin to question it. I knew I had to foster this light and that it was more important than everything else I had made important in my life. I knew it would lead me home, to the real me.

When I returned back to my life, it didn't seem to fit anymore. I knew I had to change things. I left my relationship of three years and put my company on the market. The voices around me said this was crazy, while the voice within me said, *You're doing the right thing.*

WHAT I THOUGHT WOULD MAKE
ME HAPPY DID NOT

Have you ever achieved something you thought you really wanted, only to feel unfulfilled afterward? What I thought would make me happy did not. I did all the things that I thought defined success. I built a socially responsible company from the ground up. I was featured in *The New York Times, People Magazine,* and appeared on *The Rosie O'Donnell Show.* All the things that you're told will make you happy—success, money, influence, recognition—didn't fulfill me on a heart and spirit level. I climbed the mountain I thought I was supposed to climb. When I got to the top, I realized after all the hard work, time, money, and resources I had expended, that it wasn't my mountain. I had defined success externally; I bought into the illusion. I was living someone else's idea of success. It clearly wasn't mine or I wouldn't feel so unfulfilled. I discovered the hard way that success has to come from within. When I walked away from my "successful" life, everyone thought I was out of my mind. In retrospect, it was just the beginning of learning to be. What I discovered on my journey is that we have to get out of our minds to know who we are, why we are here, and what will truly fulfill us. It is the path of being spirit led, where I discovered all my answers.

THE SPIRIT-LED MODEL

Many of us are familiar with the importance of the mind, body, and spirit connection. Yet, most of us lead our lives from our minds, not from our spirits. Even in the way we say the phrase "mind, body, spirit," mind comes first and spirit comes last, when, in actuality, we want spirit to be in the lead. Here's why: When we lead from the mind, we cannot create balance in our life because we are not connected to Source. A connection with Source brings us into alignment with our spirit. Without that connection, we often have the experience that something is missing in our lives. No matter how much we achieve, have, or do, there are still feelings of being disconnected. When we become spirit led, Source energy flows to us and through us, making co-creation possible.

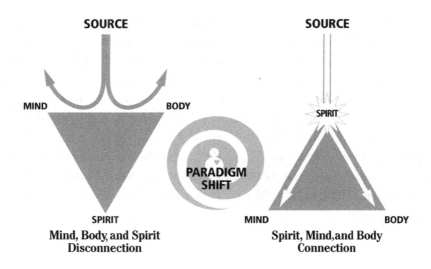

**Mind, Body, and Spirit
Disconnection**   **Spirit, Mind, and Body
Connection**

When we lead with the spirit, we are in alignment with the limitless self. From this place, the mind and body also become aligned. Source energy is able to flow as we express our true selves in the world, creating purpose and balance in our lives and giving us a direct path to co-create our greatest vision. The spirit has the power to lead us to the extraordinary, to the life that is most aligned for us. There is nothing more fulfilling than this. This is the paradigm shift that is emerging individually and globally.

Spiritual growth is what facilitates the connection to our spirit. It allows us to know ourselves in deeper and deeper ways, giving us access to our authentic desires and joy so we can experience all aspects of our lives in much more meaningful ways. Our freedom is dependent on our growth. As we peel away the layers that are our false selves, we become lighter and freer to be who we truly are. For me, a part of the false self was the identity I took on of businesswoman extraordinaire: tough, forthright, and never taking "no" for an answer. This identity wasn't really who I was, even when my mind told me it was so. By connecting to my spirit, I started to discover who I really was. This enabled me to let go of the layers of the false self. As a result, the incongruence between who I was being and who I really was began to heal. I felt freer and happier.

The peace that comes from knowing ourselves cannot be achieved externally. To live our best lives and create our own reality, we must become conscious. This is the path of working from the inside out; the path of being spirit led.

HOW TO APPROACH THE TOOLS

I want to be clear. I am not asking you to believe in anything I teach you in this book. What I am asking is that you try the transformational tools I will give you. If you have doubts, then put them away for now. Suspend judgment until you have used the tools and seen the results for yourself. I have found in facilitating spiritual work for many years that the most important thing is being 100 percent open to the experience while you are having it. The problem is, if you decide ahead of time this isn't for you, then it won't be, and you'll never really know.

Transformation does not occur by reading about it or understanding it intellectually; it happens experientially. We cannot transform without doing the work. There is no pill we can take to be spirit led. That said, it does not have to be hard, boring, or uninspired. In this book, you will find what I call Homeplay and Playsheets. You will find a Homeplay section at the end of each chapter and Playsheets throughout this book. These are exercises you can play with to help you learn the tools and integrate the transformations you are experiencing as spirit into your mind and body. This is a necessary step to transforming into your limitless self. Many of you have read books and been given practices that you never applied. This probably didn't help you transform. It is when we apply the tools that we see results. The Homeplay gives you a place to do this. Whenever you approach this process, you want to practice The Three Cs: Centering, Clearing, and Connecting (in chapter 2). Because your mind is not doing the work; it must come from your spirit. Remember, your mind has answers, but not the ones you are seeking. Let your spirit lead you to your greatest vision.

In the course of my journey as a Spirit Coach, I have seen countless clients use these simple, non-dogmatic tools and their lives dramatically change. The reason I developed these tools for my clients and, now, for you is that I want to offer you a direct path to your spirit. On my personal journey, I have spent years studying with too many spiritual teachers to mention in this book. I have developed my own intuition, guidance and healing abilities at the Foundation for Spiritual Development for over a decade. I have taught retreats, workshops, and seminars encountering and serving people from all walks of life. I have discovered through this journey of sometimes learning the hard way, tools that work, not just on myself but for many others. My hope for you is that you do not waste time, money, and resources like I did and that you will go directly to where the answers you are seeking are—within you. The first tool I am going to share with you is an important first step in the process of being spirit led because we need to learn to be out of our minds in order to hear the voice of spirit. Let's get started.

THE FIRST STEP IS TO
QUIET YOUR MIND

"Are you out of your mind?" I often say this at the beginning of my seminars. Most people laugh because they think of this as a "bad" thing; no one wants to appear crazy. Yet, exiting the mind is a prerequisite to being spirit led. This can be a difficult task without the right tools. How often do you experience monkey-mind—where you can't stop your thoughts; they just keep spinning round and round in your head? Well, for most of us, this is a common daily occurrence. If you have driven your car from one place to another and can't remember the journey, you have been experiencing monkey-mind. Imagine what you may be missing while you're driving to your destination, not to mention your entire life's journey. Learning to still your mind leads to a more focused, productive, and joyous day, but most importantly, it leads to spirit.

Sherry, one of my Spirit Coaching clients, was constantly thinking—thinking about her to-do list, her children, her job, her future... From the moment she woke up to the moment she went to bed, Sherry was thinking. As you can imagine, this made going to sleep rather difficult. Sherry couldn't stop her mind from racing, and this kept her awake night after night. She began to practice a tool I taught her where she would stop and take a minute to visualize a ball of golden light expanding in the center of her head, pushing out all of her thoughts. She did this technique before going to bed and found that it calmed her down and she was able to relax enough to fall asleep. This helped her get much-needed sleep and made her days better. Based on the great results she was getting by using this tool before bed, Sherry started to use it during the day when she felt scattered. She noticed that she became more relaxed, peaceful, and productive during her day. She later told me, "It is amazing what gets done when you are out of your mind."

This is the first transformational tool I taught Sherry and the first one I would like to share with you.

TRANSFORMATIONAL TOOL #1:
QUIET YOUR MIND

Light of Christ

1. Imagine a small golden ball of healing light, about the size of a quarter, in the center of your head. You can visualize this or just simply feel the healing light in your head expanding.

2. Let the golden light *slowly* grow until it fills your entire skull, with the intention of pushing out all of your thoughts. *filling with Jesus –*

3. Imagine the light glowing brightly and expanding slightly beyond your physical head, keeping your focus on the golden light for one minute or more. *engulfing*

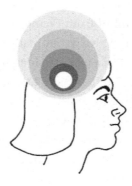

You can use this tool anywhere. It takes one minute or less and can help you begin the process of exiting your mind. The next time you are aware you are no longer present, take a moment to use this tool.

Repeat this process as needed. You will be amazed at the peace that comes from a still mind, not to mention other profound benefits.

BE FREE OF NEGATIVITY USING
THE LET GO AND KNOW LIST

Stilling the mind is different from emptying the mind. In the course of any given day, we accumulate negative thoughts and feelings: fear, guilt, shame, blame, self-criticism, anger, regret... We all do, even when we pretend we don't. Over time this negativity builds if we do not find a constructive way to release it. In fact, we carry it around with us during our day, drawing in experiences that reflect the energy that is within us. It is always in our best interest to release these negative thoughts and feelings; otherwise, we will just have more thoughts and feelings that are similar. I call this the Think-Feel Spiral. We think negative thoughts and feel bad and think more negative thoughts and feel worse and so on. We get stuck in a loop of negative thinking and feeling, spiraling downward. The Let Go and Know List is a way to break this pattern. We all know that how we feel can change the course of our day and, cumulatively, it changes the course of our life. When we let go of the negativity, we feel lighter and brighter, hold a new clarity, make much better choices, and draw in experiences that are more aligned.

I first used this tool over a decade ago, and because I received such amazing results, I use it consistently today. At the time, I was working as an independent business consultant and was fuming about a client who was really taking advantage of me. It seemed I had gotten myself into a situation where I was not being compensated for all the work I was doing. Not only that, but my client was taking credit for everything that I was creating for her.

This anger consumed me even long after I stopped working with this person. I would find myself thinking about how I had built a multimillion-dollar company and didn't have anything to show for it. It was so insidious that it would just creep in at the oddest moments: when I was brushing my teeth or driving my car or pitching a new client. It was this lingering animosity that kept my attention focused on the past. I finally decided to do something about it.

I learned this tool initially at The Foundation for Spiritual Development, where I was studying at the time of this incident. I took a piece a paper, drew a line vertically down the center, and on one side of the line, I wrote everything my past client had done to me and how I felt about it. It wasn't pretty. There was ranting and raving, even a few curse words thrown in. Then in the left-hand column, I wrote down my name, her name, and Creator. This was everyone that needed to know about this situation so I could let it go. This didn't mean I went out and told my past client about all my grievances; it just allowed me to acknowledge to myself who was involved so I could release any energy that was still connected to them. I then took that piece of paper and asked Creator to transform all the negative energy on it to love and light. And I burned it. Boy, did it feel good. I noticed right away a big weight had been lifted. Over the course of the next week, I did this a few more times.

As I was writing the list for the third time, I started to observe that this situation had happened before in my life. In fact, memories flooded in of the times when I gave everything away just because I wanted to be liked. It seemed to have been a pattern that I was just now recognizing. This all came out on the paper. I realized I had not been clear with my client. I did not set any boundaries with her. I was the one that let her take advantage of me. This process helped me become aware of and take responsibility for my part in the situation.

The last couple of times I made my list, I received Divine guidance to write on the backside of my paper, "I forgive myself. I forgive my past client. Thank you, Creator, for transforming this negative energy to love and light." And you know what? I really did. I just let go of it. It no longer plagued my thoughts. I was completely neutral to my old client. As you can imagine, this was such a relief.

God's favor

A few weeks later, something else miraculous happened. My old client called me out of the blue; I hadn't heard from her in over a year. She proceeded to tell me how much she appreciated the work I had done for her and truly acknowledged my contribution to help her build her now-very-successful company. This was enough proof for me to recognize that when we truly let go and forgive, we no longer block what it is we were wanting in the first place. I never had this situation happen again in my life. I actually broke the pattern—all because I used this transformational tool that has evolved over the last decade. I named it the Let Go and Know List.

The Let Go and Know List is a way of releasing negative energy. It has a dual purpose; the first is to let any and all negativity go, including both your thoughts and your feelings. The second purpose is to become aware of the negative energy that you carry around with you and why you let it be there. You may be unconscious that you're carrying it, but it still affects you. Even experiences that have happened in the past can affect us in the present. Many times we carry negativity from years past and don't know it is affecting us or how to let it go. This process addresses both the big "stuff" and the small daily "stuff." This tool allows for co-creation to occur. Even when we can't let go of the guilt, shame, anger, resentment, or judgment by ourselves, we can give it over to spirit. When we hand these emotions over to spirit, we will no longer be triggered by similar situations. For example, we may become enraged when people cut us off in traffic. As we release this energy constructively, using the Let Go and Know List, we no longer feel so angry when this happens. In fact, over time, the event happens less and less. This is because once we are able to let go of any negativity associated with a particular situation, we no longer attract similar situations.

TRANSFORMATIONAL TOOL #2:
THE LET GO AND KNOW LIST

1. Get a sheet of paper or copy the Playsheet provided.

2. If you are using a plain sheet of paper, draw a vertical line down the center of the page, creating two columns.

3. Label the first column: *What Do I Need to Let Go of?* and the second column: *Who Needs to Know?* (This means listing whoever is involved in the situation.)

4. Let everything you are thinking and feeling come out as you answer the question, *What Do I Need to Let Go of?* and write it down in the first column. Do not edit. It is important to include absolutely anything that comes up: fear, doubt, anxiety, situations from the past, regrets, what you don't like about yourself... It is important to release whatever negativity is there. You want to allow yourself to get to the point where you are taking responsibility for anything you may have done now or in the past. When you do this, it frees you from holding onto those negative situations any longer and helps to prevent creating similar experiences in the future.

5. In the second column, *Who Needs to Know?*, write down anyone who is involved in the situation. Your name definitely needs to be on this side along with any other parties that may have been involved, directly or indirectly. The purpose of this exercise is to clear negative energy between you and others. It is not necessary to actively engage with any of the people on your list about your negative feelings; this list is to help you take responsibility for your own energy and clean up what does not serve you.

For example:

What Do I Need to Let Go of?	Who Needs to Know?
My boss pushed his agenda onto me	my boss, me
I let him push his agenda onto me	me
I didn't say no when I could have	me
I am not valuing myself, my time	me
Beating myself up again	me
Fear of meeting today	me, my boss
Being angry with James yesterday	James, me
Feeling overwhelmed	me, my kids
Jealous of my girlfriend	Jane, me
Frustrated with my life	me, God
The pain in my lower back!	me, my body
Anything I am not aware of at this time	me, God

I forgive myself. I forgive   Jane, James, Pete, Sara

Thank you, Creator, for transforming all negativity to love and light.

6. After you have completed the list, fold it in half and write the fol-
    lowing on it (or you can also create your own): *I forgive myself. I
    forgive X. Thank you, Creator, for transforming all negativity to love
    and light.* You can say this out loud or silently to yourself. Your
    intention is to release this energy.

7. The last step is to burn or shred the list. Complete this process in
    one sitting; do not leave this laying around the house for someone
    to find. This process is for you and you alone.

The Let Go and Know List

What Do I Need to Let Go of?	Who Needs to Know?

I forgive myself. I forgive _____

Thank you, Creator, for transforming all negativity to love and light.

Go to www.spiritcoachtraining.com/playsheet for a free downloadable PDF

Feel free to repeat this process whenever you feel the need to rid yourself of negative energies. This is great to do on a daily basis. As you release this negativity consistently, you will notice that you experience less and less negative, recurring thoughts and feelings; they no longer plague your mind. Once you practice this tool, you will find that you are able to easily return to your spirit's natural state of clarity, peace, and neutrality.

I use the Let Go and Know List on a daily basis. Doing this keeps me from slipping into any predisposition for negative thinking. I am preventatively letting go of negativity. This allows me to experience more peace, joy, and gratitude for the people, places, and situations I encounter throughout my day. I find I have more energy to expend in the areas that serve me because I am no longer dwelling in the past, nor do I let any negativity stick with me in the present. This obviously results in a better day and, ultimately, a better life.

HOMEPLAY

☐ Each night before you go to bed, use Transformational Tool #1: Quiet Your Mind. Observe the results; notice if you fall asleep faster and if you sleep better. Try this consistently for a week. If it works, begin to use it throughout your day whenever you notice you are unfocused or overwhelmed.

☐ Pick three days this week to use Transformational Tool #2: The Let Go and Know List before you start your day. Observe your thoughts and feelings afterward. Notice if you feel better immediately and how long this feeling lasts. If you find this works for you, use it daily as a constructive way to eliminate and prevent future negative thoughts and feelings. If you find there is a specific situation that is disturbing you during the course of your day, stop and use this tool. This will get you back into a clear, neutral place to make your best choices.

CHAPTER TWO

FIVE MINUTES TO FREEDOM AND FULFILLMENT

"To have something permanently, you must choose it perpetually."
- P. Raymond Stewart

I walked into a store in Sedona, Arizona, with one goal: to show my clients how a spiritual practice could change their lives. To do this, I would get an accurate picture of my electromagnetic field before and after my spiritual practice. Sedona is known for the mystical, the outrageous, and even the woo-woo. You will find all kinds of chakra clearing, psychic readings, soul retrievals, and the list goes on, but what I was looking for were some hard facts. A Russian scientist named Semyon Kirlian developed a technology called Kirlian photography, a.k.a. aura photographs. Kirlian photography is a technique of photography that, with the help of high-frequency detection, displays the luminescence of an object's aura, or energy field.

I told the saleswoman I wanted two Kirlian photographs taken of me—the first one taken as normal, and the second taken after waiting three minutes. She agreed to do it without knowing exactly what I was up to. I sat down, and she hooked me up to the machine. I just focused on what I might during the normal course of the day: thinking about my to-do lists, thinking about what I might buy in the store later, just plain thinking. After she took the first picture, however, I completely changed my focus.

I began meditating using a specific spiritual practice that I teach my clients. For just three minutes, I used these simple tools that can, literally, transform you. Then, "click!" another photo was taken of my electromagnetic field, showing a much more radiant, expansive energy field.

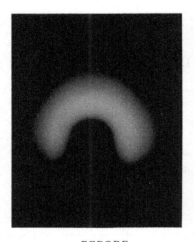 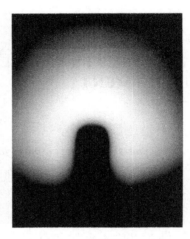

BEFORE   AFTER

What you are looking at is a headshot of me. Yes, that is my head in the middle. What is around my head, the light, is my electromagnetic field. Notice the difference between the size, shape and brightness of the light around my head before and after. My electromagnetic field went from a small, dense energy to a significantly larger, luminous, bright, and expansive field. You are looking at a black and white version. The original photos were taken in color where the difference between the two photos was even more apparent. As you can see by comparing the two photos, I significantly shifted my energy in just three minutes. In this chapter, I am going to show you how to do this, as well as what to do with the other two minutes. The truth is, a spiritual practice will transform you. This is why it is the first thing I have my clients do every day.

HOW A SIMPLE SPIRITUAL PRACTICE CAN TRANSFORM YOUR LIFE NOW

Most people don't know where to start in creating a spiritual practice, so they never begin. They say to me, "I don't have time for a spiritual practice." Sound familiar? If you want to transform yourself and your life, this is where you begin. It is what I teach first to people wanting to transform. If you have five minutes, then you have time.

Everyone can take five minutes to make their day better. Cumulatively, this creates a better life. Don't take my word for it; try it for yourself. I firmly believe in practical spirituality, meaning it has to work and be beneficial. Otherwise, why do it? You will never know if something works until you try it. Give it 100 percent of your energy for a short period of time, let's say a couple of weeks, and then decide if it is for you. With all the transformational tools I am sharing with you in this book, I encourage you to be a scientist in your own life by experimenting and observing the results. If you see positive results, keep doing it. You will receive even more benefits. If you don't see results, then stop and try something else.

What I am about to show you changes lives—not because it is so revolutionary or a quick fix, but because, over time, you become more aligned with your spirit, your true self, and infinite source of power. Nothing can take the place of the fulfillment and peace you will gain by being spirit led.

One of my clients, who owns multiple companies, told me point blank, "I don't have time for a spiritual practice; I have to work." I responded by saying, "This is your work." He looked at me strangely, but seemed somewhat intrigued. I went on to explain, "If you want work to work better, then work on yourself first. After all, you're the common denominator. If you change yourself, you change the way you experience the world and the way you impact the world around you." Then I asked him, "Are you willing to take five minutes each day for the next week to do a little experiment?" He said he'd give it a shot.

When we talked a week later, the first thing he said to me was, "I can't afford not to take five minutes. It gave me more focus, clarity, inspiration, creativity, and saved me literally hours of the day!" This client is only one among thousands who discovered the value of a spiritual practice.

Many of the people I coach are very busy. They run successful companies, some more than one at a time. They have full lives, like most of us, and believe they do not have time for a spiritual practice. When they begin with just five minutes out of their day, something significant happens. Countless times, my clients come back to me, and they say, "Jenai, I can't go without a spiritual practice because that five minutes makes a significant and measurable difference in my day." When I ask them why, they explain they are more present. They are more focused. They are more connected. They are able to see opportunities when they are presented. They experience more peace and awareness, leading them to make the best choices for them.

A spiritual practice is your first step to transforming your life and becoming connected to your spirit. The reason we need a spiritual practice is because what changes us is not reading about it or talking about it; it is experiencing it. When we have a spiritual practice, it begins to transform us on a daily basis. It transforms us by aligning us to our spirit, gradually, more and more. It helps us to access our Divine truth, letting us know when and how to act on that information. Spiritual practice creates more alignment in our lives because we tune into our truth, what's really, truly important. I think most of us are on information overload. We're always trying to accumulate more information, yet information doesn't change us. It's the application of the information that transforms us. It is experiential. When we are able to connect to our spirit experientially, we can discern what is aligned and what is not. And when we're able to discern what is aligned, we can move in that direction. This is what I mean by being spirit led. Being spirit led will save us time, money, and energy. This is the reason why my clients tell me a spiritual practice saves them hours in their day, not to mention the peace, compassion, love, inspiration, etc., that they also experience.

SPIRITUAL PRACTICE REVEALS
OUR GREATNESS

When Michelangelo was asked how he carved the *David*, he replied by saying that David was already there. What he meant was, when the giant piece of marble arrived, he only had to chip away at what David was not. The sculpture's form, its authenticity, was already there; it was innate. Just like each and every one of us—our spirit is innate. Our divinity lies within us. Spiritual practice is about the chipping-away process. Without a spiritual practice, we live in a world of illusion. We believe we are the marble waiting for someone or something to make us great, when the truth is, we already are.

Spiritual growth is not about trying to be "more spiritual" by someone else's definition. It is not about trying to be someone you are not. It is about becoming more aligned with your spirit. The thing is, you are already spirit; it has just been buried inside the layers of facades that have been built up to protect yourself. There comes a point in our life that we realize, by protecting ourselves, we actually lose ourselves. When we lose ourselves, we become unhappy, unfulfilled, and often begin to create somewhat destructive patterns to create a crack in the facade so we can find ourselves again. Spiritual practice is merely a way to begin to peel away the layers of the onion that aren't us and to discover who we are at our core—spirit.

If I could give you only one message, it would be, "You are enough." Working for many years with many different people, what I have experienced both in myself and in others is an inability to recognize we are enough: good enough, smart enough, beautiful enough…just enough. No matter how successful someone appears on the outside, there is still this lingering place within them of "not being enough."

This is what, in fact, drives the entire self-help movement. There are millions of books on how to be "better." But what if being better is not what it is about? What if we already have within us what constitutes us being "better," but are not accessing it? When we are spirit led, we actualize the best of who we are, while simultaneously understanding that we are enough.

Our minds will always have us believing there is something more, better, and bigger to achieve. This is just our disconnect from spirit and our attachment to the mind. It is problematic because there is always another goal to be reached or hurdle to jump in order for us to feel good about ourselves. And even then, it is momentary and we need the next achievement to feel good again. On the other hand, the spirit knows why we are here and what our highest choices are in each moment. It is not a competition, but rather a way of being in the world that allows for us to grow and evolve in an aligned way. The spirit path is a path of peace, authenticity, and renewal. It does not require us to be perfect, only aligned with spirit. Walking the path of spirit gives us an opportunity to move away from the duality of right and wrong. Understand that it is about being in absolute integrity with your spirit self. This inherently leads to a very high level of achievement without the need or goal of achieving.

Which spiritual path we follow is irrelevant. What is important is that we follow one. All paths eventually lead to self-mastery, and to master the self is to find one's spirit. This is what we are all seeking, whether we are aware of this or not. It is fruitless to compare your path to another's, to try to assess which is better or worse. You should only be concerned with whether you are on your own path and that you are putting one foot in front of the other.

LOOKING WITHIN TO ACHIEVE
SELF-MASTERY

I remember when I first stepped on the path of self-mastery. Of course, I was happy to be the master of anything I could, especially back then. Unfortunately, I only liked to attempt mastery if I knew I could succeed. When I quickly realized self-mastery was not my strong suit, I tried to run the other way. I always liked a challenge, like building a company or helping a friend through a horrible break-up. Strategically, though, I avoided the things I thought I wasn't good at and focused on what I knew I could accomplish. Unfortunately, all the things I seemed to be good at were external, so I ended up avoiding myself. This led to a life where I mastered many things, but not myself. And although I achieved many goals, I was somehow still not satisfied with my life. The truth is, I would never be satisfied with my life unless I was willing to look within myself.

If we are not satisfied with our lives, it's because we don't know what satisfies us on a spirit level. This is the reason for a spiritual practice. The only way I know of to get through the difficult terrain and navigate the bumps along the path is a spiritual practice—a daily practice that you do regardless of whether you want to or not.

I am not a religious person, so when I began devising my daily spiritual practice, it consisted of meditating. Now, I was a Type A overachiever, and multitasking may as well have been my middle name. When I sat down to try and quiet my mind for five minutes, it was no small feat. I started my practice with a baby step, five minutes a day, come rain or shine. In the beginning, it felt like the longest five minutes of my life. Eventually, I grew to enjoy my five minutes of peace and quiet. As I meditated, I noticed that the quality of my day changed. I became more present and more at ease. What used to be stressful no longer seemed to bother me.

Today, meditation is how I spend the first part of every day. If you had told me when I first began a spiritual practice that this is something I would look forward to and count on for the rest of my life, I wouldn't have believed you. I know now that it is the glue that holds my life together.

It always amazes me how much time and energy we are willing to put into our bodies and minds, but not our spirits. We will make the time to go to the gym or learn a new skill for our jobs, but we don't make the time to connect to who we really are. When all is said and done, the spirit is the part of us that we take with us, so why is our focus always elsewhere?

A spiritual practice brings us back in touch with our spirits. The only way to connect with this part of us is experientially. We have to be still and quiet and allow ourselves to begin to experience our true selves. This happens when we meditate. The more we are able to connect to our true selves through a spiritual practice, the more we are able to be authentic in our lives. Being authentic creates a more fulfilling life because we attract the people, the work, and the experiences that are in alignment. This brings a deep satisfaction, which cannot be found unless we are willing and able to be connected to our spirits. Otherwise, we are just seeking ego gratification and experience momentary pleasure that is not sustainable.

Michelangelo had it right. Our greatness is not something we can go out and find; it is something we already have within us. When we access this place, our spirits and beauty are revealed to the world and the world becomes a better place.

THE EVIDENCE ON MEDITATION

There have been many scientific studies on meditation. The results are extremely favorable. This book is not about the research. In fact, I believe the proof comes from your direct experience of participating in a daily spiritual practice. That said, I would like to share a few examples of scientific research, even if it is to simply appease the mind.

One of my favorite studies, published by the *International Journal of Neuroscience*, showed that people who had practiced a short daily meditation for a five-year period were biologically twelve to fifteen years younger than their actual age. Numerous studies over the course of the last thirty years have shown that meditation aids our health and well-being in countless ways. One of the pioneers in this research, Dr. Benson at Harvard Medical School, showed that meditation leads to a significant increase in relaxation and, thus, numerous health benefits. For example, it slows the heart rate, decreases respiratory rate, increases blood flow, lowers oxygen consumption, lowers blood pressure, and decreases levels of blood lactate (linked to anxiety).

Meditation affects our neurophysiology in extremely favorable ways. Some of the early scientific studies on brain wave patterns (EEG) suggest that a person who meditates cultivates the qualities of being focused, calm, and creative. In this particular study, meditation was shown to increase alpha production (8–13 Hz or cycles per second). Alpha patterns are linked to calm and focused attention. There was also an increase in theta production (4–7 Hz). Theta patterns are linked to imagery and creativity.

Meditation has been shown to help us sleep better. Remember my client, Sherry, who used a meditation technique I taught her before going to bed? One of the reasons meditation helped Sherry and can help you sleep better is that it has been identified to increase melatonin production. Melatonin, an important neurotransmitter, regulates sleep patterns, and this directly impacts our mood and behavior. Additional research shows melatonin as having immune-enhancing properties.

John Kabat-Zinn, PhD, the founder and director of the Stress Reduction Clinic at the University of Massachusetts Medical Center, conducted a study that showed how meditation is able to alleviate pain in the meditator. This has certainly been my experience.

My hope in sharing this brief sampling of research with you is that it will inspire you to begin your daily spiritual practice and stick with it.

THE FIRST THING YOU DO SETS
THE PRECEDENT FOR THE DAY

What is the first thing you do when you wake up in the morning? Before I started a daily spiritual practice, as soon as I woke, my mind went into overdrive thinking of all the things I had to do that day. These first thoughts pretty much set the tone for the rest of the day, keeping my mind in overdrive until my head hit the pillow again later that night. Then I woke up and did it all again. Once I realized that I was setting an unconscious intention for every day to be stressful by the way I began my day, I shifted the way I began my day.

Now the first thing I do every day is my spiritual practice. No, I don't check my voicemail or email, or even eat breakfast first. I know from my own experience and my experiences with many clients over the years that what we do first sets the precedent for the rest of our day. That said, I encourage you to experiment and see for yourself. At first, it was difficult for me to break out of the old habit of jumping into my day full speed ahead, but eventually I developed a new habit that was in my best interest. This is what a spiritual practice does.

Why is it that sometimes we wake up in a great mood and other days, perhaps more frequently, we feel like we have been run over by a truck, deflated and lackluster? Fortunately, we do not have to leave it up to fate; we can control our own energy, thoughts, and feelings. We can't control anything else, but we do have dominion over our internal landscape. Without the right tools, it may seem impossible that we can actually be in charge of how we think and feel. When we have these simple tools for transformation, which I am about to share with you, we become empowered to transform our lives by transforming ourselves.

CARVING OUT YOUR SACRED SPACE

I find that the reason many people don't take the time for a spiritual practice is that they have not yet created space for it in their lives. They have not made the time, but I am also talking about the physical space. Where are you going to do your practice? It is important to define this ahead of time. Where will you go to be alone, uninterrupted, and feel safe during your five minutes? It is about creating something that works for you. I have a client who has a large family and finds that the only space that works for her is in her large walk-in closet. She set up a chair and an altar inside, and it has become her private sanctuary. It is important to determine exactly where is best suited for you to begin your practice. You could choose your bed, but this may not work if you fall back to sleep. I recommend designating a place, outside of your bed for your spiritual practice.

When I first began meditating, I had very little space. I decided to buy a special chair and place it by the window, and this was my spot to meditate. I designated the chair as off limits for everyone else in my household. It had one purpose only: It was the container for my spiritual practice. Seeing it every day reminded me of my commitment to myself and inspired me to do the work. You may want to play inspiring music, light a candle, or create a special altar for yourself. That said, none of these things are necessary. Do not let setting these things up be an impediment to beginning your own practice.

THE THREE Cs:
CENTERING, CLEARING, AND CONNECTING—
YOUR FIVE-MINUTE PRACTICE

Without the right tools, a spiritual practice may seem difficult. The tools I am about to share with you are known as active meditations; they utilize imagination as a technique. For some of us, to imagine means to visualize; for others, it means to feel or sense. Whether you feel more comfortable seeing things or feeling things with your imagination does not matter. Eventually, as you practice the tools, you will develop your intuitive muscles in all areas. Many of us have tried passive meditation and then believed meditating was not for us. Passive meditation is focused on quieting the mind. This, however, can be difficult if the mind does not turn off. Sometimes, no matter how hard we try, it still keeps interfering. After a while, we end up feeling like we failed. Active meditations give the mind something to do and a way to focus so it does not interfere in the process. Eventually, it just gets out of the way altogether. This is how you train your mind to get out of the driver's seat and let the spirit lead.

The active meditations I am going to teach you are called "The Three Cs." There are three parts to the practice: Centering, Clearing, and Connecting. Your first tool is Centering.

TRANSFORMATIONAL TOOL #3:
CENTERING—YOUR GROUNDING CORD

1. Imagine what the center of the earth looks like to you. It could look like a solid ball of rock, a crystal, or anything that you imagine to be a strong anchor for you.

2. Next, visualize and/or feel a strong, sturdy tree trunk with a beam of white light in the center. Let this beautiful tree trunk encompass your entire rib cage, front-to-back and side-to-side.

3. See this tree going all the way down through your physical body, through the floor, and through all the layers of the earth.

4. Let the roots of the tree wrap around the center of the earth, what you imagine to be your anchor, several times, connecting you to the healing energy of the planet.

5. Continue visualizing and/or feeling this tree connecting you, rooting you, and grounding you until you have the sensation of being grounded and rooted in present-time.

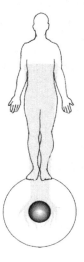

To be centered in your self is to be completely present. This means you bring 100 percent of your energy here, in the now, which is the most powerful place to be. Without the right tool, this can almost seem impossible to achieve. You may be present for one moment, and then the next moment you are thinking about that meeting you have to attend later today. When you are thinking about the future or thinking about the past, you are not in the present. The result is, your energy is dispersed. Whatever you are doing in the moment takes more time, energy, and focus because you are not centered. This tool has been revolutionary for many of my clients. The results they get from being present are not only key for more clarity, focus, and attention, but without it, they were literally missing large portions of their lives.

SOME BENEFITS OF CENTERING

Being centered brings you out of the past or future into the now; the now is where you will find everything you are looking for. Being centered helps you make choices without fear, anxiety, or worry. As centering connects your body to the earth, you connect to the life force of the planet, which gives you more energy and vitality. It brings your brain into an alpha state. Alpha patterns are associated with calm and focused attention. This tool helps you feel safe. As you ground into the earth, you connect to your strength, wisdom, and courage. When you are present, you are paying attention; you do not miss the opportunities presented to you. Through your own practice of using centering, you will discover in what ways it benefits you.

Here is how centering helped someone at a retreat I facilitated several years ago in the Canadian Rockies. The group and I were about to board a helicopter to take us to the resort where the retreat was being held. There was one problem—one of the participants was terrified of helicopters. There were no roads to where we were going; the only way in was to fly. I didn't want this person to turn around and go home, so I worked with him to help alleviate his fears. When I asked him what scared him about flying, he told me, "When my feet are not touching the earth, I feel disconnected. This creates anxiety for me."

I had the perfect tool for him. I explained to him that a grounding cord connects him right into the center of the earth, whether he was standing right on the earth or flying above it 15,000 feet in the air. He looked at me as if I was a little crazy, something I was quite used to at this point.

Standing there on the ground, I had him close his eyes and imagine a beautiful redwood tree trunk was wrapping around his ribcage, expanding way beyond his physical body. The tree trunk went through the ground and through all the layers of the earth until it wrapped its roots around the center of the earth.

I asked him how this felt. He explained that he felt calmer and less afraid.

"Great," I said. "Now, I want you to do the same thing while you are in the helicopter."

I have to admit he was a little wary but did it anyway. The entire way there, he practiced the grounding cord tool I had shown him.

When we arrived at our destination, he was elated—not because he made it there in one piece, but because for the first time in his life, he hadn't felt afraid while flying. He conquered his fear by using this tool. He also continued using it as part of his five-minute spiritual practice, which I taught him later during the retreat.

TRANSFORMATIONAL TOOL #4:
CLEARING—YOUR SPIRIT BUBBLE

After Centering, the next step in your active meditation is Clearing.

1. Imagine a bubble of clear white light surrounding you. It starts in the center of your body and expands slowly outward until it reaches about five feet in all directions: above, below, behind, and in front of you.

2. Feel the bubble around you, 360 degrees, focusing your intention on pushing anything out that is not aligned. All the stuff you have in your energy field is being cleared so you can have a calm, peaceful vibration.

3. Take a moment to focus on your Spirit Bubble radiating this clear, white light. Make sure it is extended equally behind you as it is in front of you. Notice how you feel your own energy is enhanced, while at the same time being protected from outside energies that you may not want in.

No matter what is going on around you, you are energized and protected in your bubble of light, consciously choosing how you want to feel. The intention you are holding is that what is aligned with your highest good can enter your bubble, and what is not is deflected. If, for example, you are around someone who is very negative, that energy does not need to affect you. In fact, it just bounces off your bubble. Conversely, when someone is sending you love, you allow it in, enhancing your energy.

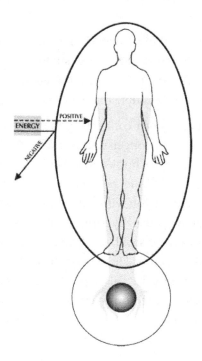

SOME BENEFITS OF CLEARING

Clearing changes your energy from bad to good or good to better. It helps you stay protected without being an emotional sponge. It gives you the ability to choose what energy you want to experience (and what you don't). As you use this tool, your energy begins to vibrate at higher frequencies, attracting in more aligned experiences and deflecting what is not aligned for your highest good. This tool is part of your spiritual practice, and you can continue to use it throughout your day to receive all these benefits and more. Try it for yourself and observe the results.

Like the man attending my retreat, I, too, had fear in certain situations. In my case, it seemed that whenever I was walking in downtown San Francisco, the weirdest of the weird would approach me. It appeared I was a magnet for crazy people. Looking back on it, I realize I was just too energetically open. I would welcome in anything—the good, the bad, the ugly—and they all came. When I started using my Grounding Cord (Centering) with my Spirit Bubble (Clearing), things changed for me almost instantaneously.

On one occasion, I was walking down Market Street, and I could see yet another "crazy guy" on the other side of the street eyeballing me; he was headed directly toward me. I started to brace myself like I normally would, but then I remembered I had a couple of new tools.

I imagined my grounding cord connecting me deep into the center of the earth. I immediately felt stronger and less afraid. Then, I visualized clear, white light filling my entire body and beyond until it went out about three feet in front of me, behind me, below me, and above me. I suddenly felt different, more powerful, if you will. The crazy guy who was making a beeline directly to me at an unusually rapid pace stopped suddenly a few feet from me and took an abrupt step back. It was as if he hit my Spirit Bubble and it knocked him backwards. He then proceeded to walk around me, swerving a few feet to my left side. This was all I needed as proof that this tool works. Now I don't leave the house without it. And I stopped being a magnet for what I didn't want.

You can use this tool to stop attracting what you don't want. As you can see, this tool can be used not just as part of your designated spiritual practice, but throughout your day. Not only does it deflect what you do not want, but it helps you attract what you do by creating a clear, peaceful energy within you.

TRANSFORMATIONAL TOOL #5:
CONNECTING—YOUR CONNECTION TO SPIRIT

The third step in The Three Cs of your active meditation is Connecting.

1. Visualize or feel a golden light pouring down into your bubble, sometimes like a gentle rain and other times like a waterfall, depending on what is comfortable to you.

2. Let the golden light permeate your head, neck, and shoulders, and work it all the way down to your feet and beyond your physical body.

3. Visualize this gold light as Source energy filling and connecting you. It may help you to imagine this light as radiant sunlight. Allow it to gently wash away anything that is not authentically you, releasing it down through your grounding cord. This may include limiting beliefs, negative feelings, and even pain in your body.

4. Let the light of Source illuminate the spirit in you. This is being Connected.

5. Let yourself receive this healing energy for the rest of your five minutes. Simply relax and enjoy the feeling that comes with a radiant expansive energy field.

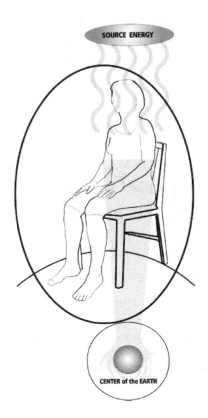

SOME BENEFITS OF CONNECTING

This tool connects you to your spirit, the Divine in you. It quiets the mind, clearing stress and negativity, helping to eliminate negative and limiting beliefs, thoughts, and experiences. It moves you ahead in your spiritual growth, becoming a process of chipping away your false self. It also enhances your intuition, resulting in increased focus, clarity, and discernment. It fills you with radiant Source light, so you become a healing presence to yourself and others.

When my grandmother died, I spoke at her funeral. Despite the best efforts of my logical mind to detour me, I guided everyone at the standing-room-only service through a very brief meditation. I was not so certain if my New York relatives would appreciate this gesture coming from the "woo-woo" granddaughter from California. I asked everyone to center themselves by visualizing a strong, sturdy tree grounding them safely into the center of the earth. Then, I asked everyone to visualize the love they felt for my grandmother as a color that they imagined pouring down over them like a gentle waterfall. I asked that they continue imagining this for several minutes. My intention was to bring some peace to the pain many of us were experiencing due to the physical loss of my grandmother. An hour later, I was in the limousine driving to Long Island where we were to bury my grandmother and say our final goodbyes. It had been eerily silent for some time when my grandfather broke the silence by asking, "Who was it that said at the funeral home to imagine the color of love?" I gulped, fearing I may have upset my grandfather even more than he already was. "It was me, Grandpa," I said gingerly. He responded quite matter-of-factly, "That is the first time in a long time I have felt peace in my heart. Thank you."

Of course, I will never forget this experience and how it taught me the importance of not only having a spiritual practice, especially during difficult times, but following our intuition, even in the face of fear. When we do, we serve others.

Doing a simple spiritual practice daily on a committed basis can change your life. One year after I made a commitment to myself to meditate every day, no matter what, my life had taken a completely different course. I had drawn in the love of my life, was beginning to do my life's work, began communicating with my guides, and found a deep inner peace. Knowing that I was consistently practicing The Three Cs helped me discern the best choices for me. Of course, I did not stop there. I knew this was a prerequisite for being spirit led, and I was committed for the duration.

Most of the people I coach do not need as long as I did to see significant changes in their lives. One client, after a few weeks, began writing a screenplay—it just flowed out of her. Another discovered his life purpose and began taking action on living it. Another client after just three months began channeling Christ Consciousness. He had never even meditated before he began working with me. One of my clients says it best: "A spiritual practice is one of those things that makes ten things happen." Your first step in living a spirit-led life is beginning a daily spiritual practice.

TIPS FOR DESIGNING YOUR OWN SPIRITUAL PRACTICE

- Keep it simple

- Decide where you will meditate

- Start with five minutes a day

- Make it the first thing you do each day

- Experiment with music

- Practice The Three Cs

- Be still and you will begin to know your spirit

- Be open to your spirit's guidance

- Afterward, observe the results

TOP 10 REASONS WHY A SPIRITUAL PRACTICE WILL BENEFIT YOU

1. By doing a daily practice, you begin to discover the real you.

2. If you can't spend time with yourself, why would anyone else want to?

3. Learning how to be, instead of just doing, gives you the ability to have more by doing less.

4. You no longer have to seek answers outside of yourself.

5. Connecting to Creator allows you to become a co-creator (Now who's powerful?).

6. You gain clarity and a greater ability to discern what is true for you.

7. You learn to listen to your intuition (the voice of your spirit) to make more aligned, fulfilling choices.

8. You cultivate compassion and love for yourself and others.

9. You experience an innate joy that is not dependent on anything external.

10. You see yourself as spirit having a human journey. This allows you to be in the world but not of it.

There are plenty more reasons why it is beneficial to start a spiritual practice, but what I want to know is, what are yours? After doing your five-minute spiritual practice for one week or more, I'd love to hear why you keep doing it. You can let me know by going to www.facebook.com/spiritcoachtraining. If you would like access to a free meditation that guides you through the process of The Three Cs, called Five Minutes to Freedom and Fulfillment, go to www.spiritcoachtraining.com/5-minutes-to-freedom-and-fulfillment.

HOMEPLAY

☐ This week, pick two or three days to do your five-minute practice. If you need to, set a timer. Practice The Three Cs: Centering, Clearing, and Connecting. Observe the difference between the days you did your five-minute practice and the days you didn't. Be a scientist in your own life. You can even record your results. Next week, try the five-minute practice every day. Over time, you will notice it has a cumulative effect.

☐ If you find, during the course of your day, you are distracted or thinking about the past or future, use Transformational Tool #3: Centering—Your Grounding Cord, to bring yourself back to present time.

☐ Before you leave your house, you can use Transformational Tool #4: Clearing—Your Spirit Bubble, to enhance the positive and minimize the negative, while feeling safe and powerful in your own space.

☐ After a while, you will notice you look forward to Transformational Tool #5: Connecting—Your Connection to Spirit, because it nourishes you on a deep level. Over time, you will find your connection to your spirit getting stronger and stronger.

CHAPTER THREE

How to Do Less and Be More While Discovering the Real You

"The universe is not asking us to do something,
the universe is asking us to be something."
- Lucille Clifton

I ntention is such a powerful tool that when we put our attention on intention, life begins to shift almost immediately. Mike, a psychologist by training, went to a workshop to learn about intention. He thought it might help him in working with his clients. What he didn't realize was that it would impact him personally and change the course of his life.

At the time, he was having severe marital problems with his wife of thirty years. In fact, he was seriously considering leaving her. Mike was terribly conflicted inside, as he knew this was not the relationship he wanted to have, but he was willing to work on it if there was even a slight chance the relationship could be saved. As a last-ditch effort, Mike thought he might apply the tools he just learned in the workshop to his marriage, without being cognizant of how powerful they actually were.

Being a scientist, he decided to conduct a controlled experiment in which he would record the results of each day. To create the control, some days would need to be like any other day, with no unusual activities, while on other days he would apply the tools of intention. He chose the odd days of the week not to do anything differently and the even days of the week to apply intention.

The even days began with him getting up in the morning and meditating. After meditating, he would ask his spirit who he needed to be that day. These were specific qualities he would focus on throughout his day. It was usually something like being appreciative, present, and loving. Then, he would write down all the things he loved about his wife. At first, this was very difficult for him, as he couldn't remember what he loved or even liked about her. In his imagination, he would go back to when they first met 30 years before and remember what it was like when he fell in love with her. He decided to do this practice twice a day, once in the morning and once during his lunch hour.

Immediately, he noticed a difference. He began to feel happier about himself and less apt to pick apart his wife. He also noticed on the days that he practiced this technique, his wife was happier and easier to be around. In contrast, on the days he didn't practice this, when he arrived home from work, his wife was often nowhere to be found and when they did interact it was always abrasive. By the end of the week, he noticed on the even days that he and his wife were actually getting along. They sat down to dinner, and for the first time in what seemed liked years, they laughed together.

This was astonishing to the doctor, and he wanted to share what he was doing with his wife. He felt a little bit dishonest experimenting without her knowledge, but he realized he had to tell her if it could save their marriage.

When he described what he had been up to the last week, his wife had a look of intense relief on her face. She told her husband she thought she was going mad. She went on to explain that, on the odd days, she felt very depressed and low, but somehow, on the even days, she began to feel happy and hopeful about life. The roller-coaster ride of emotions was driving her crazy. In her new awareness of what had actually been happening, she realized that they were so connected that his intentions were affecting her. And they agreed it also worked the other way around.

They both decided that day to put into practice the power of intention. Each day, they did the same intention exercises Mike had been doing on the even days. One day at a time, they repaired their marriage. They are still together, enjoying each other and truly living happily ever after.

WHAT IS INTENTION?

Intention is allowing our spirit to direct things. Most of us allow our minds to lead. This simply means our thoughts and actions determine the results we are experiencing. The problem with this is, if the mind is driving us, we will not end up at the highest and best experience for us. Why? Because the mind cannot know what our highest and best experience is. It is just a tool to actualize the directives of spirit. We have made it the primary self. It believes it is the leader and leads accordingly. Let's put it this way. If the mind is driving the car, we will often go in circles; things may look different, but in actuality, it is the same patterns we have experienced before. The only way to change the results we are experiencing is to allow the mind to take a backseat and let the spirit drive. When we let the spirit lead, we consciously create the best results in the easiest way.

Since the mind is about action, about bringing things into fruition in the world, it would have us believe that thinking about action and doing action all the time is the best way to be. After all, we live in a "just-do-it" world; everything we are taught is about action. Of course it is important to act, but to act without a clear directive from spirit, without intention, is just busyness. We have all been swept up in busyness. It seems that there is never enough time, energy, or money for what we are creating. It will always take more of all of these resources when we are just acting from the mind.

Thoughts play a key role in all of this. "What we think about, we bring about," is a common expression in the self-help movement. To a certain extent, this is true, but not completely. Positive thinking aids us in the results we want to create. However, positive thinking alone will not get us where we want to go. Why? Because it is intention that directs our thoughts. Why is it that even when we think repeatedly we will win the lottery, we don't? We may imagine winning over and over again in our mind, but we still don't win. Thinking alone will not create the results we want. It is, however, part of the process. When we work from the perspective of our spirit, we are working from intention; this is what directs everything. When we are spirit led, suddenly we are able to know how to direct our thoughts and actions to experience the results that are aligned for us.

This does not mean you will win the lottery, unless it is your spirit's path. The spirit will create your highest and best path when you follow it. However, it may not look exactly like you think it should. This is where trust comes in. Without trust, working at the level of intention is impossible.

I used to believe intention was all about action; that is, intention was something that you did. This is a limited definition of intention, although it speaks to how many people live their lives. They have a plan about how it should be or how they would like it to be, but often this plan is unsuccessful because it lacks alignment with spirit. Sometimes we can't see the big picture, but we believe we can. We create a plan or set of actions that are about the result we want to achieve. This negates co-creating because we are not open to the possibility that there may be another way to achieve the result we want that is more in alignment with who we are. "We make plans and God laughs" is an old saying that describes what happens when we are not spirit led. Intention is using our spirit to direct our thoughts and actions, co-creating the results in alignment with our highest good.

Working at the level of energy is another way of describing using intention. When we understand that this part of ourselves—our spirit—is energy, we begin to realize that everything in the universe is also energy. Intention is working at the level of energy; this is the foundation of the universe. Learning tools like The Three Cs help us direct our own energy and the energy around us, allowing us to work at the level of intention. The least amount of energy and effort is required because we are tapping into a power much greater than our individual selves. In essence, we become a co-creator with the Divine in us, and the Divine in all. This requires us to sync with the Divine plan, and trust it.

TRUST YOUR TRUTH

You can never have too much trust in your Self. I use a capital "S" in Self because this is your spirit self. We equate who we are with our minds, when, in fact, the mind is only a tool through which we filter reality. If we identify ourselves only with our minds, what we create and how we create is very limited. The problem with going along through the years and ignoring our spirit is not only that we are not led down the path most aligned for us, but also that we stop trusting our spirit self. Every time we hear our spirit but ignore it, it sends a signal that we do not trust it. Eventually, the mind takes over and we just stop hearing spirit altogether. Our intuition is our spirit speaking to us. If we ignore this voice, we become disconnected from the part of our self that is infinite and can lead us to fulfilling our spirit's true path.

At first, you may hear your spirit as a small, subtle voice, but the more you listen, the louder it gets. Do not judge the answers you receive, even if they don't make sense. In fact, if they don't make sense, you know they are not coming from your mind. The language of our intuition is just that—a language. It takes time to understand it. The good news is you were born fluent, so it won't be long before you remember. When you apply the transformational tools in this book, you will automatically become more intuitive. The more you use it, the more it grows. As it does, you will expand your ability to be spirit led.

At any point, we can make a commitment to our spirit by listening and following our inner guidance. Every time we do, we expand our capacity to trust our spirit self and move forward on our spirit's path. This is the beginning of living a spirit-led life.

HOW TO BE IN A "JUST DO IT" WORLD

Learning how to be, instead of just doing, gives you the ability to have more by doing less. Gandhi said, "Be the change you wish to see in the world." What was he really saying? He was teaching us that it is who we are being that creates our experience of reality. If, for a moment, you can contemplate how one man transformed a nation by being the peace and justice he wished for his country, you can see that the results were nothing less than a peaceful revolution. If there is an example of understanding the power of intention, it can be found in Gandhi's legacy. Spirit led is what Gandhi was. It was here that he found his power, and the same is true for you. Intention is not something you do; it is a way of being in the world.

Most of us decide on a result we want and then ask what we need to do to achieve it. I did it this way for many years. It takes an awful lot of effort to make things happen this way. I spent years running a "successful" company, but I was exhausted and knew this method of creating was not sustainable. I vowed to myself to find a better way. Being the change is the way. My mantra has become "Just Be It" and the rest will follow.

INTENTION CHART— HOW TO USE IT

What does this mean in practical terms? Look at the chart below:

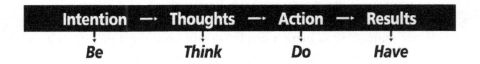

Intention →	Thoughts →	Action →	Results
Be	**Think**	**Do**	**Have**

Working at the level of intention is first and foremost about being conscious of who we are being (Intention), what we think (Thoughts), what we do (Action), and the result of this is what we have in our lives (Results).

Most of us do the opposite; we decide the result that we want to have and then ask ourselves what we need to do to get it. We go directly into action. Action is an important step, but it is also effortful and often unproductive unless you take action from the position of intention. Some of us believe, if we change our thoughts, then we can create the result we want, but many of us are still ending up with the wrong result. Why? Because intention is what directs our thoughts. When we create from intention, we realize action is not the first step in the creation process, but the last step. When intention directs our thoughts and actions, we are working at the level of energy. This requires the least amount of effort possible. Our results become an extension of who we are being.

For example, if I want to clean my garage, I need to ask myself who I need to be in order to have a clean garage. I may need to be focused, persistent, and decisive. If I am being these qualities, the result I want (a clean garage) will manifest. Intention is a way of being in the world. It is qualitative as opposed to quantitative. The next time you decide what you want (Result), instead of asking what you need to do (Action) to get it, ask yourself who you need to be (Intention) to have it.

Let me tell you about a woman who attended one of my retreats—her name is Judy. She is a strategic management consultant. She is always directing groups, managing others, and looking at the big picture. When she attended my retreat, she was having a hard time focusing on herself. After all, she was always the leader, worrying about everyone else. When I asked her what result she wanted, she said it was to leave this retreat with a new vision for her life. I had everyone set their intention at the beginning of the retreat and write it down on their name tags so they would not forget. Judy's intention was to be peaceful, inward, and connected to her spirit. In fact, Judy's intention was so powerful that when the group was moving into a different exercise, Judy was completely oblivious; her focus was solely on herself. I had to go over and tap her on the shoulder to get her attention. This was a great change of pace for her to be directed inward, and as a result of her intention, she left renewed with a clear vision of her spirit's path.

Now I use intention on a daily basis because I know who I am being will co-create the results I want with the least amount of effort. Sometimes we think we know what we want, but we don't. Think is the operative word, as it is mind-based, meaning our wants are coming from mind. Being spirit led allows what we want to come from spirit. The way to access this is by Centering, Clearing, and Connecting. Each morning after practicing The Three Cs, I allow my spirit to direct my intention by asking who I need to be today. Usually two or three qualities emerge, and I write them down at the top of my to-do list, knowing full well that who I am being will result in what I accomplish that day. It never ceases to amaze me how my spirit-directed intentions are completely accurate and help me co-create a better day.

TRANSFORMATIONAL TOOL #6:
SET A DAILY INTENTION

1. Set your intention at the beginning of your day. The best time to set your intention is after you meditate; this is when you are clear and most aligned with your spirit. After you have practiced The Three Cs, ask your spirit for two to three intentions for the day. These are qualitative, who you want to be today.

    Here are some actual examples from my clients who set their intention in the morning and then reflected on the results at the end of their day:

    My intention today is to be: *present, guided, and connected to my spirit.*

    Results: "I accomplished so much today because I was so present. I felt guided all day. I even bumped into a colleague who I haven't seen for a long time who agreed to help me with a project I am working on."

    My intention today is to be: *abundant, open, and receptive.*

Results: "I noticed people seemed friendlier. I also received a free item at the grocery store after being charged the wrong price. I won $13 at work from a $1 raffle ticket that I had forgotten I had purchased."

My intention today is to be: *grateful and joyful.*

Results: "I was aware of the little things that I might normally take for granted. I took my car in for repairs; it ended up being half the cost they had told me it would be."

2. Write down your intention for the day and put it where you will see it throughout your day. "My intention is to be…" This could be on a sticky note, at the top of your to-do list, or on your computer or phone. You can even write it on a small piece of paper and put it in your pocket.

3. Reflect on your intention throughout your day. This will remind you of who you need to be to co-create your best results today.

4. Observe the results and write them down.

DAILY INTENTION PLAYSHEET

Record your intentions on the Playsheet on the next page. Make sure you observe the results and write them down. This will reinforce your ability to use this tool successfully.

DAILY INTENTION PLAYSHEET

Day One
My intention today is to be _____

Results _____

_____

Day Two
My intention today is to be _____

Results _____

_____

Day Three
My intention today is to be _____

Results _____

_____

Day Four
My intention today is to be _____

Results _____

_____

Day Five
My intention today is to be _____

Results _____

_____

Day Six
My intention today is to be _____

Results _____

_____

Day Seven
My intention today is to be _____

Results _____

_____

Go to www.spiritcoachtraining.com/playsheet for a free downloadable PDF

When we consciously use intention, our spirit directs our thoughts, the words we speak are our truth, the actions we take emanate from who we are, and the results we create lead to success as we have defined it. By using intention, we are co-creating what we want; we are inspired, or in-spirit, and everything we think, speak, and do inspires the world around us. It is not only easier to co-create, but life is more fulfilling because it is emanating from our spirit. Our visions and dreams are effortlessly propelled into reality.

WILL THE REAL YOU PLEASE STAND UP?

Now that you have your Daily Intention, it is important to create more "Be Time" for yourself. It is often difficult in our day-to-day routine to see the big picture of our lives. Even when we get the opportunity to have some downtime, there are still phone calls, emails, errands, and the whirling dervish mind that is constantly reminding us of all the things we need to do.

I have a client who scheduled himself in half-hour segments, rarely giving himself any time when he was not doing something. In fact, even when he went on vacation, it took him several days just to settle into his newfound freedom and be present. Unfortunately, just when he was able to let go of work, he had to turn around and go right back to it. I suggested to my client to schedule some Be Time. This meant he would actually add to his daily planner, "12 p.m. to 1 p.m.—Be Time." In that hour, he would sit and do nothing. Yes, absolutely nothing. This was very difficult for him at first, as you can imagine. As John became more familiar with Be Time, he noticed he was calmer, more relaxed. Eventually, he began to notice he was much more creative after taking Be Time. In fact, it was so apparent to him that he intentionally scheduled it in before doing any new development on his projects.

You may be thinking, Why would I want to waste my time doing nothing? The answer is simple: The time is not wasted. Without learning to be, you do not know who you really are. We are not human *doings*; we are human *beings*. Until we can be with our spirit and like the company we keep, we will not know how to love, how to live, and what truly makes our heart sing. Be Time is a critical component in a spirit-led life. The irony of Be Time is that it saves you time. When we take time to be, we are taking the time to learn about who we are. Without this awareness, we go through life by default, trying this and trying that, to discover what it is we wish to create. By *being*, we embody fully who we are and all of our choices are an extension of this.

Another benefit of Be Time is it changes our perception of time. Time is relative. It slows down or speeds up according to our perceptions of it. If we are running around like a chicken without a head for most of the day, time seems to speed up in conjunction with our acceleration. If we are on vacation and have nothing to do or nowhere to go, time appears to go very slowly. When we consciously slow down, we actually increase the amount of time in our days, or at least the perception of time; this makes us feel relaxed and calm. As a result, we find we become much more productive. This is not the way most of us view it; we believe if we can just move faster, do one more thing, and multitask, we will get more done in a given day. This seems logical, but it is ultimately ineffective. That is how I used to live my life—how most of us live our lives. We wake up and the rat race begins. Our perception is that there is never enough time. The key is: Change our perceptions and we change our experiences of time.

TRANSFORMATIONAL TOOL #7:
CREATE "BE TIME"

1. Set the day and the amount of time you are committing to practice Be Time, *prior to starting*, and schedule it in. Start with ten minutes and slowly give yourself more time as you get more comfortable with it.

2. Pick a place to do this that is nurturing for you. For example, in your garden or at your favorite park. Practicing Be Time in nature is always preferable, but if you can't be outside, find a comfortable, quiet spot inside.

3. Turn all phones off or, better yet, *leave them behind.*

4. Give yourself permission to let go of any agendas.

5. Set your intention, for example: *to be quiet, calm, and fully present with my spirit.*

6. Do not bring any distractions: books, music, *definitely not your cell phone.*

7. Bring a pen and a pad to write on. You may have a breakthrough, ideas, and even epiphanies. You can record these. If you do not, this is okay, too. *It is best to have no agenda.*

8. Practice observing without thought, without cataloguing what you see. Simply notice what is happening around you without any judgment.

TIPS FOR CREATING "BE TIME"

Giving yourself permission to unplug from everything, even the ones you love, for a short period of time, is nothing less than renewing. It helps you notice where you have been and where you would like to go. It lets you become connected again to the spirit that lives within—you know, that small subtle voice that we often ignore. When you are connected to spirit, it is impossible to ignore. This is the beauty, because when you start listening to that voice, your world blooms with colorful ideas of how to live better. Like a spring garden, the possibilities are born again.

Start with ten minutes and then work your way up to a full day. I realize some of us just do not have three days to create a personal retreat, but if you do, I encourage you to take it. That said, even when you don't have a large block of time, you can always schedule some Be Time. You get to decide the when and where of it. It could be a morning spent alone on your favorite mountain or an afternoon at the beach or even ten minutes in the park.

Know that you will emerge from Be Time renewed and restored, ready to rejoin the world, and perhaps just a little bit more connected to the spirit in you. Take Be Time often and you will find your entire perspective changes to one of awe and gratitude that you get to live this amazing life. You may even notice how much more present you are for everyone you love and everything you are creating. You will most certainly realize that you are not alone in your creations as you walk in the world, spirit led instead.

HOMEPLAY

☐ Each morning after you practice Centering, Clearing, and Connecting, ask your spirit what your intention for today is using Transformational Tool #6: Set a Daily Intention. Make sure it is no more than two to three qualities. Write it down somewhere and carry it with you. Look at it throughout your day. At the end of the day, reflect on how this intention served you. Practice this for at least a week. If you notice positive results, keep using it.

☐ Look at your calendar and decide where to block off some Be Time using Transformational Tool #7: Create "Be Time." Start with ten minutes.

☐ Slowly work your way up to an hour. If you really feel adventurous, schedule in a personal retreat for yourself, taking one to four days. Notice how you feel after your Be Time. Do you feel more energized, creative, inspired? If so, keep scheduling it into your life.

CHAPTER FOUR

THE POWER OF INTEGRITY TO LEAD YOU TO YOUR HIGHEST VISION

"Secure your own oxygen mask before assisting others."
- Airline take-off instructions

Getting in integrity with myself changed my life. It all started in therapy. Being raised by two therapists, I was no stranger to psychoanalysis; I had my first session at the age of five and used it on and off for most of my life. So when I found myself unhappy in my late twenties, I sought counsel in the familiar, a therapist. Her name was Dr. Megan, and unbeknownst to me, she was no ordinary therapist.

I arrived in her office and began to talk about "my problems." No more than five minutes had elapsed and she exclaimed, "Why are you here?" Catching me off guard, the question stopped me in mid-sentence. In all my years of therapy, no one had ever asked me this question in a way that insinuated therapy would not give me what I was looking for. Dr. Megan, taking my jaw hanging half open as an opportunity to talk, told me point blank, "You don't need therapy!" Then she began to describe my future. "You are going to be working with people to help them awaken to their

Divine potential, to empower them to live extraordinary lives… you are going to be teaching and facilitating groups." She said this very matter-of-factly, "You are here to do very important work." Then she continued, "You need to develop your gifts. I recommend attending classes to open up your intuitive and healing abilities." Then she said, "And by the way, do you want to use my office for teaching groups? You can use it for free."

I was a bit flabbergasted by Dr. Megan's remarks and unwavering certainty. At the time, I was a business consultant and didn't have a clue what "awakening Divine potential" was. Even though my mind had no idea what she was talking about, my spirit resonated with the truth she was telling me. I later learned I was in the presence of a psychic psychologist and light worker. I left her office and began the process of getting in integrity with myself, which created a turning point in my life.

It had appeared that for the majority of my life I was not living in integrity. Yes, I was ethical with others, always showing up when I said I would. When I made them, I would keep agreements with family, friends, and business associates. For the most part, I thought I was a person of integrity. However, I was not showing up for me, following my truth, keeping agreements with myself, and walking the path of spirit. My life changed after my brief meeting with this unusual therapist. She reminded me that if I was not in integrity with my spirit then I was actually not living in integrity at all; without this, I was certainly not going to live the life I came to live.

In this chapter, you will see how integrity is listening to and following your spirit. You will learn tools to clean up the areas where you are not in integrity with yourself. When you do, there is nothing that can stop you from living your highest and best life. We have all heard the expression, "The only thing that is getting in your way is you." Being out of integrity with yourself is what is getting in your way, and it does not need to be the case anymore.

WHAT IS INTEGRITY?

Integrity is the ability to be aligned with your spirit, where you can access your truth and act on it accordingly. This creates a sense of wholeness, trust, and the energy needed to co-create anything. The word integrity literally means wholeness; to be whole is to be in integrity. When we are operating solely from the mind or body, we are not whole. We have left out the most important part of ourselves: spirit. It is no surprise that if we are not being spirit led, we will not have the ability to know our truth in its entirety. In fact, it is impossible to be in integrity with ourselves without this connection. That feeling that is always there, lingering in the background telling us that something is missing, is our lack of wholeness. It is who we are, our spirit. Once we recognize this, we begin the journey back to wholeness. When we are whole, we experience fulfillment.

Everything in our lives that we are trying to create has a direct relationship to being in integrity or not. All the places in which we are not will become energy drains that do not allow us to create the lives we want to live. There is nothing more important than being in integrity with ourselves. If we aren't, then who will be? Everything we create in this world is a direct result of being in integrity with ourselves or not.

We are taught that when we make an agreement with someone, we should always keep it. But what happens to the agreements we make with ourselves? These are usually the ones we break the most often. We feel that when we put ourselves at the center of our lives, we are being selfish. However, there is a difference between being selfish and putting our self at the center of our lives. Selfish is hoarding, greedy, and not thinking about how our actions or inactions affect others. Putting ourselves at the center of our lives is actually where we are meant to be.

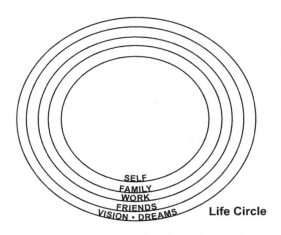

Life Circle

YOUR LIFE CIRCLE

Imagine putting yourself at the center of your life. Yes, you are not putting your work, your friends, or even your family ahead of you. You are placing yourself at the front and center of your life; this is where you are meant to be. The outer rings of your Life Circle may be different for you than someone else. This depends on your individual priorities, and they are important for you to define. However, you will always be at the center of your own life when you are willing to put yourself there. You will find when you prioritize yourself first that you have more to give others, in all areas of your life. After all, you are not an extra, but rather the star of your own life. When you let spirit lead, you also become the director.

Take a moment to visualize your Life Circle as a three-dimensional cup. Imagine the places you are out of integrity with yourself as holes that appear in the bottom of the cup or the center of the Self Circle. What you would like to create in your life does not manifest because these Integrity Holes make it difficult to create your vision and dreams, and as a result, you are constantly losing energy through the holes. When this is happening, everything you do feels like it is just about surviving—no matter how much you try, you cannot thrive in your life. So much of what we are trying to create, the big picture, falls through the holes. It is no wonder that life can sometimes feel overwhelming.

It is important to realize that we all have holes. We are holey, as well as being holy. It is part of the human experience. The process of discovering your holes is not meant to be more fuel for beating yourself up. In fact, for most of us, this is an integrity hole that needs to be addressed. Wasted energy happens when we spend our time and precious energy beating ourselves up. Like any energy drain, we can outline a step-by-step, simple strategy to get rid of this behavior. Some of the Integrity Holes we will need to address will be internal, such as self-criticism, judgment, anger, ignoring our inner guidance, not taking time to develop our gifts... And some of the holes will be external things, such as taxes, cleaning the garage, making amends with someone in our life... Whether it is internal or external, you will find, as you repair the holes, you no longer have the energy drains attached to each issue. You can be free to expend your energy elsewhere in more aligned and productive ways. I just want to note here that I find, when we work more closely on the internal holes, the external ones automatically work themselves out. This is because the world reflects to us what is going on inside of us. Once we start to clean up the holes, suddenly we have more energy and we begin to see the manifestation of our vision in the world.

For example, one of my clients, Jackie, had been divorced for about ten years, yet her ex-husband was still a source of much stress and discord in her life. Every time her kids had an important event, her ex would not show up, and her kids would be disappointed. This was upsetting to my client. Jackie realized when she was identifying her Integrity Holes that this was an energy drain for her. But what could she do about it? After all, you cannot change someone else.

I encouraged Jackie to look at her part in this situation. She was baffled at first, but then realized she had never really forgiven her ex-husband. She was still carrying around a lot of anger and animosity. Jackie decided that she needed to forgive him and let go of worrying about the choices he was making. Jackie used a series of Let Go and Know Lists focusing solely on her ex; it took several. She also meditated and asked for help in forgiving her ex-husband. Then, she created a pattern interrupt, so every time she had a negative thought about him, she would say the word "cancel," as if to erase that thought. This process only took a couple of weeks to shift a destructive pattern of being angry and resentful toward her ex, not bad for a decade or more of wasted energy.

The most interesting thing that happened as a result of Jackie's ability to get in integrity with herself and forgive her ex was that her ex started showing up more often for the kids. Suddenly, he made it to more events and began changing the way he approached her and the kids. This was a great lesson for Jackie. She had believed she needed to change her ex when all she had to do was change herself. When we change, the world around us changes.

I have another client, Sara, who was always overbooked, overworked, and overwhelmed. There was simply not enough hours in the day to get everything done that Sara needed to do. She believed that was just how it was and did not realize that there was a big Integrity Hole that she was not willing to address. This hole was her inability to say "no." She didn't believe she could say no to things. To every colleague, parent, friend, teacher, associate, and community member who asked her to do something, she would say, "Sure." This led to a life out of control. Sara never had time for herself, let alone the time to pursue her vision. Sara had to learn to simply say "no."

Together, we devised a simple three-step plan to patch up this Integrity Hole. The first step was to have Sara practice saying "no." It really was hard for her to even say it, as if it were a dirty word. She felt she was disappointing others every time she said it. The second step was to find a constructive place to let go of her overwhelm, fear of change, and worries about disappointing others so it wouldn't affect her choices. This is what a Let Go and Know List is for; she did a few of these.

The last step became discernment. How would she know what to say "yes" to and what to say "no" to? She needed to discern what was aligned for her and what was not. She used a tool (which you will learn later in this chapter): she would replace "should" with the word "choose." Every time she thought she should do something, she would ask herself if she was choosing to do it or not. Right away, she could tell if it was true for her. Suddenly, she had a discernment tool. When she did choose something, she did it with 100 percent of her energy. She stopped doing all the shoulds.

This opened up space in Sara's life for the real "yeses." She suddenly had time for herself and her dreams by patching up just one Integrity Hole.

TRANSFORMATIONAL TOOL #8:
HOW TO DISCOVER YOUR INTEGRITY HOLES AND REPAIR THEM

1. Make sure you practice Centering, Clearing, and Connecting before you start this process. This way, you will be spirit led and will be aware of what to address that will give you the most benefit at this time.

2. Grab a piece of paper and pen. You can also use the Playsheet provided.

3. Create a list of three items you need to address. This may include looking at different areas of your life, such as relationships, work, health, financial, community, spiritual, play, etc. You are the common denominator in all those areas. By addressing the three key energy leaks, you will find that all the areas of your life benefit. I am not asking you to address everything at once. This would be too overwhelming for anyone. What I would like you to do is simply pick three key Integrity Holes.

   For example:

   I am out of integrity because *I don't listen to my intuition enough.*

   I am out of integrity because *I judge myself and others.*

   I am out of integrity because *I don't say "no" to the requests in my life that are not aligned for me.*

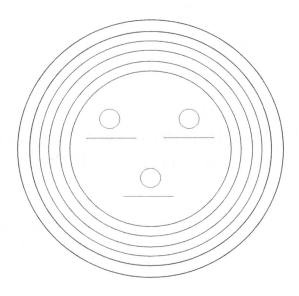

4. Now that you have identified three holes, you will take each one and break it down into three baby steps. By baby steps, I am talking about very small, doable items that you can easily apply in your day-to-day life.

For example:

I am out of integrity because *I don't listen to my intuition enough.*

The steps to get back in integrity with myself are:

1. Start a five-minute practice of Centering, Clearing, and Connecting.

2. Set a Daily Intention to be present, open, and attentive to my intuition.

3. Write down every time I listen to and follow my intuition in my Evidence Journal. An Evidence Journal is just that, a journal in which you log examples of when you used your intuition and it steered you in the right direction. This builds evidence for your mind so it can let go and trust your spirit. This will reinforce your ability to use your intuition and trust it.

5. Now you have nine baby steps to take. You won't take these all at once, but rather, you will pick one per week to work on. That's it, just one simple step per week.

   For example:

   The one thing I will do to be in integrity with myself this week is:

   Set a Daily Intention to be present, open, and attentive to my intuition.

6. Now you have nine simple steps you can take to get back into integrity with your self. There is no need to do them all at once. Just pick one item on which to focus per week. As you do this, you will find your life changes. The energy you need is there, and what you thought was an impediment to your vision is not. Each week, choose one new baby step to focus on.

INTEGRITY PLAYSHEET
1. I am out of integrity because
The steps to get back in integrity with myself are:
1
2
3
2. I am out of integrity because
The steps to get back in integrity with myself are:
1
2
3

3. I am out of integrity because	
The steps to get back in integrity with myself are:	
1	
2	
3	

The one step I will take this week is:

Go to www.spiritcoachtraining.com/playsheet for a free downloadable PDF

Within three weeks, you will have cleaned up one major energy drain. This has a snowball effect on your life. As you begin filling up the holes, you will find it creates more energy to address some of the other areas that are out of integrity in your life that you have been putting off or avoiding. Suddenly, you feel free to really go for it. This, in turn, gives you the momentum to actualize your vision in the world.

Often, when we go through the Integrity Process of identifying our holes, it will bring up natural emotions, such as anger, resentment, self-blame, pain, loss… you get the picture. The key is to not let these feelings stop you from looking. This fear is what has gotten in your way before. However, now you have the tools to constructively release any negative emotion that may come up for you, allowing you to stop avoiding looking at something because you do not want to feel bad. This is when you get out the Let Go and Know List and you use it. Release anything that is coming up for you so it does not become an impediment to moving forward to live fully in your life. My suggestion is that you use this tool daily while working on repairing your Integrity Holes.

When you release the energy that is not serving you, you are able to stop manifesting in the physical what you don't want and begin manifesting what you do want. Sometimes, however, you may find that you don't have the time to write out a Let Go and Know List or you are in a situation where you don't have a piece of paper and pen handy. This is why I would like to offer you an additional tool that gives you similar results. The Rose-Release Mediation is the perfect tool when you need a quick way to release negative energy that is arising in the moment. There is nothing you need to use this tool other than a couple of minutes.

TRANSFORMATIONAL TOOL #9:
ROSE-RELEASE MEDITATION

1. Take in a deep breath of peace and hold it. When you exhale, allow everything in you that is not peace to go out with your breath. Repeat this a few times.

2. Imagine a tree trunk connecting around your ribcage and grounding you into the center of the earth, bringing yourself to present time.

3. See and/or feel your clear white Spirit Bubble expanding around you, five feet in all directions.

4. Imagine filling your Spirit Bubble with clear white light.

5. Imagine a giant rose outside of your Spirit Bubble; it is open and expansive, ready to receive what is not serving you.

6. Place any low vibration thoughts and feelings (anger, fear, confusion, judgment...), situations, people, unknowns, to-dos, etc., into the rose. Either out loud or silently, say what you are placing into the rose. Just when you think you are done, see what else may be there. This is how you get to the root cause of why you may be feeling bad.

    For example:

    My boss being critical of my performance, my mother-in-law irritating me, fear around not knowing the outcome of my career, feelings of guilt from eating too much, not getting enough sleep, self-criticism, believing I am not worthy...

7. See and/or feel any remaining negative energies as the color red, light up inside your bubble, and place it in the rose. The red is energy that we may not be conscious of at this time, but we can still release it.

8. At the count of three, imagine the rose is exploding into love and light, releasing and transmuting all negative energy.

You can use this meditation in the moment; it only takes a minute or two. When you recognize you are feeling bad, this is a quick and convenient way to release the energy that is not serving you.

SECURE YOUR OWN OXYGEN
MASK BEFORE ASSISTING OTHERS

"Secure your own oxygen mask before assisting others." I had heard flight attendants say it a hundred times before. After all, I spent most of my time traveling. She said it again, and unbeknownst to her, my entire perspective transformed. This epiphany happened exactly when I needed it. I was not yet even thirty and felt I might burn out any day. I knew my lifestyle was not sustainable. I was traveling all over the world exporting our products. I was speaking at conferences and being interviewed by radio and television. Yes, I was seemingly living the good life, yet I forgot one simple little piece of wisdom that was allowing my life to spin out of control: "Secure my own oxygen mask before assisting others." What profound wisdom. It was as if a giant light bulb went off in my awareness. This was it! My students and clients who know me now are used to me repeating this to them like a mantra.

Why might this also be important to you? When is the last time you promised yourself something and you didn't do it because someone else demanded your attention? When this happens, not only do you not get to the things that are important to you, but you stop trusting yourself. Every time we break an agreement with ourselves, our trust in ourselves erodes. Over time, this leads to not believing in ourselves. As a coach, I find that when my clients learn to believe in themselves, there is nothing they can't do. That said, every time we don't listen to that inner guidance, to our spirit telling us the way, we move a little bit further down the wrong path. I did it. You probably do it. Each time we do, we lose the ability to connect to our spirit. Integrity is like a muscle; it atrophies when we do not use it. This is the bad news. The good news is that, at any point, we can start building the muscle of integrity again.

Learning to listen and trust our truth is the key. When we do this, we become in integrity with our spirit. We learn to trust this part of our self. Sometimes, however, it is difficult to discern between the mind and the spirit, meaning we have so many "shoulds" in our head that we may be doing things for the wrong reasons. Our spirits will not lead us astray, but you bet our minds will. How do we discern between the two?

Imagine what would happen if that constant nagging voice that says, "I should get more work done, I should clean the office, I should take that new client, I should…" went away. At the very least, it would create a lot more empty space in our heads. Perhaps it is exactly the space that is needed to be more inventive, to create anew, like an artist who approaches his clean white canvas on which to create his masterpiece. I think most of us have become so accustomed to the voices in our head that tell us what we should do that we have forgotten that we get to choose.

The shoulds are like software programs that just keep running—eventually we forget why we were running them in the first place; they simply run us. Even when they have initially been put in place for a positive result, they can eventually become a hindrance instead of a help. If your "should" program is still running you, you may be caught in a lifestyle that is exhausting and unsustainable. There is a way to break out of this cycle.

The first step in winning the battle of the shoulds is awareness. If we are not aware of the programs that run us, how can we stop them? It is similar to when we first learned to drive and had to pay attention to every detail: our foot on the gas pedal, both hands on the wheel, our attention focused on the road ahead of us. Now when we drive, it is as if we are on autopilot; we no longer have to think about how to drive the vehicle. In fact, we often eat breakfast, talk on the phone, and browse the newspaper, all while driving. The problem with this is, if we stop paying attention, eventually we have an accident. An accident is a hard way to get a wake-up call. What if we started paying attention as if our life depends on it? It does. If we just start paying attention, we begin to realize we have choices.

What if we replaced every "I should" with "I choose?" The first thing that happens when we do this is we now have a discernment tool. We can immediately tell by replacing "I should" with "I choose" if something is in alignment for us or not. Is the reason we are doing something for someone else because we think we "should," or because it actually is in our best interest? Creating this type of discernment in your life will lead to more time, more energy, and the ability to make better choices.

For example, on a regular basis, I would think to myself, "I should clean my house." As I became aware of this thought, I consciously replaced the word "should" with "choose." "I choose to clean my house." Immediately, I can tell by the resonance of those words whether it is in my best interest to clean my house in this moment. This is discernment. Yes, the house may need cleaning, but is right now the optimal time? If it is, great, I will know it. Not only will I know it, but I am choosing it. When I choose to clean the house, it gets done faster and more efficiently than if I am doing it because I believe I should.

When you replace "I should" with "I choose," you immediately become more empowered. "I should" is disempowering. It drains you and takes your energy away, whereas "I choose" takes the power back to where you are owning it, taking responsibility for your choices, and bringing 100 percent of your energy to it. When you choose something, you are not doing it because you have to or you are supposed to, but because you are choosing to. It is the difference between someone telling you to do something or choosing to do something on your own, even if the person telling you to do it is yourself. Just take a moment and say the words, "I choose." Feel the power culminating within you. In contrast, say the words, "I should." Now, feel the energy draining from you. This is what happens every time you use "should," either out loud or in your thoughts.

Once you begin to liberate yourself from "I should," you begin to experience a new kind of freedom to discern your truth and follow it. Choosing your thoughts and words carefully will increase your discernment and energy levels and lead to a life you choose. This is the reason I developed this transformational tool. Let's exercise our free will; the results are nothing less than freedom.

TRANSFORMATIONAL TOOL #10:
REPLACING "I SHOULD" WITH "I CHOOSE"

1. Think of something that you believe you "should" be doing more of in your life. Say this out loud.

   For example:

   I should *visit my family for the holidays.*

2. Now, replace "**I should**" with the words "**I choose.**"

   For example:

   I choose *to visit my family for the holidays.*

3. Then say it out loud to yourself. What do you become aware of? Observe what it feels like when you say it. Does it resonate as true for you? Or does it feel untrue? Let your spirit guide you. It knows

what is best for you and the best time to do it. Remember, not choosing is also a choice.

For example:

I choose *to visit my family for the holidays.*

What did I become aware of? I don't have to go home for every holiday, only when I choose to. I noticed I don't resent my family and have a much better time when I choose to be with my family on the holidays, versus when I feel I am doing it out of obligation.

4. Once you become aware of your choice, bring 100 percent of your energy to that choice. Own it and watch the action you take get done more quickly and better than ever, while actually enjoying the experience.

Here is a Playsheet you can use to practice this tool. I suggest writing down what you believe you "should" be doing and then replace it with you "choose." Observe what you become aware of when you do this. Then, jot down what you noticed. Writing this down helps you integrate the tool and makes it more effective when you use it.

GET RID OF THE "SHOULDS" FOR GOOD PLAYSHEET	
1. I should	
I CHOOSE	
What did you become aware of?	
2. I should	
I CHOOSE	
What did you become aware of?	

3. I should	
I CHOOSE	
What did you become aware of?	

4. I should	
I CHOOSE	
What did you become aware of?	

5. I should	
I CHOOSE	
What did you become aware of?	

Go to www.spiritcoachtraining.com/playsheet for a free downloadable PDF

Practice this tool regularly in your daily life. Your ability to discern your truth and follow it will increase as you use it. Before long, you will trust yourself more and more. When you believe in you (your spirit), nothing is impossible.

THE AMOUNT OF COMPASSIONATE CONFRONTATION EQUALS THE AMOUNT OF SIMPLICITY IN YOUR LIFE

In this chapter, I have been asking you to confront yourself. Understand that without confronting the areas where you are out of integrity, you will remain stuck in the same old patterns. If you have started to clean up your Integrity Holes, you have been confronting yourself; you are already practicing a key spiritual principle, which, when applied, will make everything in your life much easier. The amount of compassionate confrontation equals the amount of simplicity in your life. The degree to which you are willing to address something in your life that is not in integrity will result in the degree of simplicity you experience. For example, if you do not pay a $25 parking ticket, over time, the fee will increase to $300. And if you still do not pay the ticket, eventually your car will get impounded and you must pay a lot of money and complete the necessary paperwork to get your car back. You have taken a simple $25 parking ticket and turned it into a complicated mess. I know—this happened to me. I am sure you have a comparable story to share.

In the past, we may have had to learn these lessons the hard way, but now we know tools that can transform our experiences in life; we no longer have to learn this way. We now know our avoidance of things will always result in having to deal with many more complications. Our willingness to face situations as they happen will result in simplicity.

When we do not compassionately confront ourselves by cleaning up our Integrity Holes, we end up living a life that is not fulfilling because we are not following our truth. This truth is dictated by spirit. Following our truth is the simplest way to live. Initially, there may be many things to compassionately confront, but after a while, we will find the path of least resistance is following our truth. This happens when we are in integrity. It is our spirit that will lead us there. When our life is spirit led, devoid of complications because we have cleaned up our holes, we have the time and energy to focus on our vision.

HOMEPLAY

☐ This week, identify the three holes you want to work on from Transformational Tool #8: How to Discover Your Integrity Holes and Repair Them. Then come up with three simple, doable steps for each hole. You only need to pick one to focus on this week. Each week, pick a new one and watch yourself get back into integrity with your spirit. From here, manifestation is easy.

☐ If, while you are doing the previous process, you notice negative feelings about yourself emerging (which, by the way, is completely normal), then use Transformational Tool #9: Rose-Release Mediation. If you find you are still beating yourself up, it is time to do the Let Go and Know List. Don't let any negativity build up and create resistance to getting back in integrity with your self.

☐ This week, also start practicing catching yourself when you are "shoulding" yourself. As soon as you notice a verbal "should," replace it with the word "choose" (Transformational Tool #10: Replacing "I Should" with "I Choose"). As you become more aware, you can begin to watch when your own inner thoughts say "should." Once you start applying this tool at this subtle level, you will find you start choosing your life much more consciously and the energy you have to live it to the fullest just keeps increasing.

CHAPTER FIVE

CHANGE THE WAY YOU SEE THE WORLD AND THE WORLD CHANGES

"An understanding of your vibrational nature will make
it possible for you to easily, deliberately create your own reality...
for there is nothing that you cannot be, do, or have."

- Abraham

I was late, arriving way behind schedule at the airport to catch a plane to Ontario, Canada, where a bus full of people who were attending the retreat I was facilitating would be waiting to take me to a resort in the Rockies. At the check-in counter, the very long line was not moving at all. Fear welled up in me. "I can't miss my flight!" I said to myself. Then my thoughts began listing all the negative possibilities that could happen if I did miss it. This went on for several minutes, until I caught myself.

I recognized I was putting my focus on all my negative feelings and that this was causing my vibration to tank. Making a conscious effort to change the situation, I began to shift my vibration by doing a Rose-Release Media-tion—yes, right then, standing in the line. After all, it wasn't really moving, anyway. I closed my eyes and visualized letting all my fear and all my other negative feelings go into the rose. Then I began to focus on what I was grateful for. It started out small, like the air I was breathing, and eventually worked its way up to being grateful that I was living my calling, doing the work I loved to do.

Five minutes later, I was feeling pretty good. I began to visualize this good feeling as a color and started sending it through me and down the line of people, all the way to the check-in staff and beyond. Another few minutes passed. Suddenly, the line went from a crawl to a steady flow. I made my flight with five minutes to spare. More importantly, I practiced what I preached and was reminded of an important lesson—*choosing my vibration is the key to transforming my experience.*

YOU CAN CHOOSE YOUR VIBRATION LEVEL

Changing your vibration is a way to change your perspective and, ultimately, your life. It is like the difference between looking through dark, foggy glasses and looking through crystal-clear glasses. By changing your vibration, you change the way you see the world. When you change the way you see the world, the world changes.

Many of us pay close attention to what we are wearing on any given day. We want to know: Is it in style? Is it appropriate for the situation? Does it make me look good?

These are the questions we ask. In fact, over the course of a year, we spend a large chunk of time, energy, and resources on the way we look. Yet, most of us give much less attention to the energy we are vibrating out into the world.

Our vibration will determine a peaceful, joyous life or a miserable one. What do I mean by vibration? We know from one of the world's great visionaries, Albert Einstein, that everything in the universe is energy, including you and me. Energy vibrates at different frequencies. Each frequency can affect you in either a positive or a negative direction. A great visual example of this can be found in Dr. Masaru Emoto's groundbreaking work in micro cluster water and Magnetic Resonance Analysis technology. He discovered that water molecules respond to the vibrations we send to them. If we think loving thoughts of gratitude, the water molecules form perfect crystals. Conversely, if we think negative, fear-based thoughts, thus vibrating negatively, the water molecules become dispersed and misaligned. His work shows us visually that our energy, when vibrating positively or negatively, will impact the world around us. This happens because each of us has an energetic field that interacts with other energetic fields. We can consciously change our energy field by raising our vibration.

Where in your life are you not vibrating at the level of peace, joy, and fulfillment? Your vibration does not come from outside of yourself, but from within. It is not dependent on who you are with, what you are doing, what deals you make, or waiting for something great to happen to feel good. Your life starts now, in this moment. In each new moment, you can make a different choice about how you would like to experience it. You choose your vibration—the level at which your energy vibrates or resonates. Are you focused on anger, or are you focused on joy? What are you choosing to dwell on? Is it fear or is it love? You may be stuck in traffic and become frustrated, beginning to vibrate at lower levels, or you may look out the window and marvel at the trees on the side of the road, raising your vibration by appreciating the beauty around you. You get to choose! In this chapter, you will learn to cultivate more awareness about your choices. You will learn how to consciously raise your vibration. You can live and feel exactly how you choose.

Cultivating awareness about what raises your vibration and what causes it to drop can mean the difference between a stressful, exhausting day and a peaceful, energized day. If you are not aware, you will likely make choices that don't serve you. By becoming aware, you can identify what drains your energy, leading to a lower vibration, and what gives you energy, leading to resonating at a higher vibration. As you eliminate the energy drains and focus on the energy givers, your vibration rises naturally to a higher frequency. You feel better, and you attract higher vibrational experiences into your life.

I have a client, Phil, who finds himself waiting for his wife on a regular basis. This is a constant energy drain for him. He is a stickler for being on time, and it annoys and frustrates him that his wife makes him late. On one such occasion, Phil and his wife were taking their three boys to Phil's parents' house and escaping for a much-needed weekend away. Their first destination was massages for two; Phil thought this would be a wonderful way to decompress from their stressful lives. Phil had gotten all three kids in the car, which is no small feat, and was again waiting for his wife, who was still in the house. His body began to tense up as he imagined each minute ticking by was another minute of the massage he was missing. He found himself getting angrier and angrier, allowing his mind to imagine every time he had ever waited for his wife. Suddenly, he was losing hours, days, and weeks off his life when he could have been doing something positive, like relaxing. By the time Phil and his wife got to the massage appointment, Phil's body was holding so much tension that it would take three days of constant massage to get him back to where he was before he began experiencing this particular energy drain.

Now, Phil believed the solution was to fix his wife from being late, but I bet if this were achieved, Phil would still find something else in which to get tense about. Let's face it, many things happen in life that are out of our control and the only choice we have is how we decide to respond to them. After a few coaching sessions, Phil realized he couldn't change his wife but he could change himself. He decided to focus on the way he reacted to waiting for his wife. Phil's initial concern was all the time he had lost in which he could have been doing something positive. Instead of using the time to get tense, angry, and frustrated, he decided he would use the extra time to relax. So, he began meditating whenever he found himself in a situation where he was waiting for his wife. He specifically focused on using the tools I had taught him, Centering, Clearing, and Connecting. These few minutes spent practicing The Three Cs became an energy giver instead of the energy drain that was happening when he was fixated on his wife making him late. It was like a breath of fresh air for Phil that ultimately changed the quality of his day. It also improved his relationship with his wife, as Phil no longer felt anger, but more love and patience for his wife.

This, in turn made it easier for her to be more relaxed as well.

Interestingly enough, over time, Phil's wife got better about being on time. She was no longer wasting energy worrying about her husband being angry with her if she was late. As a result, she could focus much better on what she needed to get done instead of worrying about what her husband was doing.

TRANSFORMATIONAL TOOL #11:
TURN ENERGY DRAINS TO ENERGY GIVERS

1. List what things drain your energy. This cultivates awareness about what activities may not be aligned for you to be participating in, or perhaps you will recognize the way you approach the activity may need to shift.

2. Then, look for a solution for each drain. The solution that you come up with will give you energy.

For example:

	ENERGY DRAINS		ENERGY GIVERS
1	Beating myself up	1	Focusing on what I am grateful for
2	Working first thing in the morning	2	Watching the sunrise before work
3	Multitasking	3	Focus on one task at a time
4	Lunch with Rebecca	4	Cancel lunch and take some "Be Time"
5	Working weekends	5	Take one day off to play outdoors
6	Sitting in traffic	6	Listening to inspiring audio-books in the car

3. Then, put your focus on the Energy Giver side of the list, practicing these items. The goal is to eliminate energy drains from your life while filling your day with energy givers. It is important to recognize we always have a choice; this happens once we become aware.

TURN ENERGY DRAINS TO ENERGY GIVERS PLAYSHEET			
ENERGY DRAINS		ENERGY GIVERS	
1		1	
2		2	
3		3	
4		4	
5		5	
6		6	
7		7	
8		8	
9		9	
10		10	
11		11	
12		12	
13		13	
14		14	
15		15	
16		16	
17		17	
18		18	
19		19	
20		20	

Go to www.spiritcoachtraining.com/playsheet for a free downloadable PDF

Sometimes, when we do this process of identifying our energy drains, we will find that no matter how hard we try, there is an energy drain that does not seem to repair. In this circumstance, we are probably missing something. This is when forgiveness, the next tool I am going to share with you, can be applied to stop the energy drain and really set you free.

FORGIVENESS IS FREEDOM

In looking back on our lives, we carry a lot of self-blame, guilt, and thoughts of "could've, would've, should've" done this, that, or the other thing. In retrospect, we can almost always think of ways we could have handled any given situation better. And yet, in the moment, it was the best choice we could make at that time. Of course, hindsight offers us many options. This is what learning from our experiences is about. In fact, there are no mistakes, only lessons to learn.

The problem with life's great lessons is that our mistakes become an impediment if we let them. You may understand in retrospect that you had a choice and you chose the wrong one. This becomes something we hang onto, and when we hang onto the past, it affects us in the present. We use these wrong choices as a reason to beat ourselves up. Unfortunately, this keeps us locked into a cycle of violence against ourselves. This will continually drain our energy and result in a much lower vibration level than is healthy for us.

It is important to know that, when we make mistakes in the past, we have the opportunity to make different choices in the present. This does not mean that we do not make amends for our wrongdoings. We do, but then we must let go of them. If we choose to hang onto them, we are in danger of recreating them in the future. Letting go requires forgiving ourselves and others because forgiveness is what ultimately releases us from our past. Forgiveness (for give) is for you to give to yourself. It has nothing to do with the person that you are forgiving; it is completely and utterly for you. Forgiveness is freedom, liberating us to vibrate at much higher levels of peace and joy.

FIVE STEPS TO FORGIVENESS

1. **Awareness**. Becoming aware or conscious that forgiveness is freedom and that, to be free, you must forgive yourself, and then others.

2. **Release**. Release all energy necessary for you to forgive. Even if at this point you cannot forgive yourself or another, you can ask your spirit and Creator to assist you in releasing any energy that keeps you tied to the past.

3. **Learn**. Learn from your experience. Once you begin to understand what the lesson is that you can take away from your experience, you begin to create forgiveness.

4. **Allow**. Allow yourself to have forgiveness. When you are able to acknowledge you deserve forgiveness, then you allow yourself to have it for you, and then for another.

5. **Be**. Be forgiveness. Once you can completely forgive yourself, you can then be forgiving of others and you can ultimately be free.

TRANSFORMATIONAL TOOL #12:
FORGIVE FOR GOOD

1. Cultivating Awareness

    Pick a person and/or situation you need to forgive and describe it below:

    _____

    _____

    _____

    _____

2. Release

   Use a Let Go and Know List to release all your negative thoughts and feelings around this person and/or situation.

3. Learn from Your Life Experience

   In each situation that requires forgiveness, we must be willing to take responsibility for our part in it. Until we do, we cannot forgive ourselves.

   What do I need to take responsibility for and forgive myself for?

   _____

   _____

   _____

   _____

   What did I learn through this experience?

   _____

   _____

   _____

   How can I make a different choice now?

   _____

   _____

   _____

   _____

4. Allow Forgiveness

Can you imagine forgiving yourself? _____ yes _____ no

Can you forgive yourself? _____ yes _____ no

Will you forgive yourself? _____ yes _____ no

If you answer "no" to any of the above questions, go back and do steps one through four again. Don't worry if you have to do this more than once—it is worth it. The results will set you free and raise your vibration considerably.

5. Be Forgiveness

Complete the following statement:

I forgive myself for

_____

I forgive

_____

Add in the person/situation you need to forgive.

How will forgiving benefit me now and in the future?

_____

_____

_____

_____

After you complete this process of forgiveness, notice how you feel. Are you vibrating higher now? As you go through the rest of your week, become aware of how letting go of this person or situation has freed you to not only feel better, but to also allow you to put your energy into more positive endeavors.

One of my clients did just this. She recognized that she resented her mother for most of her life. Mary did not have an ideal childhood. In fact, it was fraught with turmoil, alcoholism, and neglect. She had always resented her mother for not giving her what she needed as a child. This created a huge amount of animosity that Mary carried around with her. Mary and her mother rarely saw each other, and when they did, it was stressful and overwhelming for Mary. Now, Mary could not change the past, but she could learn to forgive. I coached her through the forgiveness process that I developed for just this type of situation. We used the Forgive for Good tool above, and Mary worked through it several times. Each time, she felt better, but it wasn't until the last time when she really experienced true freedom.

Mary found forgiveness for her mother and realized she had learned a great deal from her upbringing, even the parts that had caused resentment. She was able to recognize that, as an adult, she had so much more compassion for others because of her childhood experiences. As the result of forgiving her mother, she also noticed that she no longer would explode in rage at things that happened in her life that were out of control. For Mary, it was a huge relief to no longer carry around so much anger; she did not have to worry anymore about it coming out inadvertently and hurting the people who were in her life.

Another unexpected positive result occurred as well. Mary's forgiveness made room for a new relationship with her mother to be born and they began spending more time together. There no longer was that inner conflict Mary had experienced, and her mother responded positively to this change. The bickering stopped. They laughed together more. They began sharing in an intimate way and became friends. Mary is so grateful for the relationship she now has with her mother. It is the one she always wanted, and using the transformational tool, Forgive for Good, led her there.

GRATITUDE IS THE GROUND
BENEATH A MASTER'S FEET

Once we forgive, we find a huge amount of gratitude appears—much like the gratitude Mary found for her mother. After letting go of our energy drains, replacing them with energy givers and forgiving in the places we need to, we just plain feel better. This process naturally raises our vibrations, and we begin to appreciate life much more. When we are appreciating the people, places, and situations around us, our vibration skyrockets. This is why a daily practice of gratitude is so important.

I remember my thirtieth birthday; I was a wreck. I could barely hold back the tears as I was getting ready to attend a small gathering of friends being held in my honor. I didn't know how I could show up at the party like this, so sad and depressed while everyone was "happily" wishing me a happy birthday. All I kept thinking was this was not how I wanted my life to be at thirty! It was not the picture I had imagined. I felt disappointed, angry, and certainly not in the mood to celebrate.

It was a good twenty-minute drive to where the party was being held, and I needed a miracle to arrive there in a better place than I currently was in. I decided to spend the entire twenty-minute journey saying out loud all the things I was grateful for. It started out quite basic, like, I am grateful for the car I am driving that gets me from point A to point B. I am grateful for the air I am breathing. Gradually, it became more about my great health, my creativity, my ability to learn and grow. Ten minutes in, I was feeling like a completely different person. By the time I arrived, I felt completely blessed that I had the good fortune to live the life I was living. And I walked into the party ready to celebrate, but not before I thanked God for gratitude.

Gratitude is a natural state when we are being spirit led. The mind, however, will tell us otherwise. This is why when we embark on the path of spirit; practicing gratitude is central to getting our minds on board. With gratitude, there is an understanding that challenges are blessings, that failures are gifts, and that our teachers come in many forms. In the grace of gratitude, we become who we were always meant to be.

We have a choice in every moment to see the glass half full or half empty; it is always our choice. When we exercise our right to be grateful, all that we cherish emerges true and unblemished, and all that does not serve us fades away. Gratitude gives us a way of being in the world that is fundamentally positive, and this is the momentum that leads us to actualizing our vision in the world. Did you ever meet a visionary who was not grateful? Visionaries are inherently grateful, as they know their vision is part of a co-creation with spirit and without this connection spirit-led vision is not possible.

As a Spirit Coach, one of the most common predicaments I run into is people having a hard time appreciating themselves. No matter how much "success" they have had, there is still some part of them that believes they are not good enough. One of the keys to transforming this is practicing gratitude towards self. I developed this tool to assist my clients in not only learning to feel better about themselves, but beginning to embrace self-love.

TRANSFORMATIONAL TOOL #13:
GRATITUDE LIST WITH A TWIST

1. Take a medium-sized journal and title it "Gratitude Journal."

2. Then fill an entire page every day with kind, compassionate, loving, and, most important, truthful words about all the things you love and appreciate in your life. You may need to start with the basics, depending on how you feel. There is always something to appreciate. For example, I always appreciate that I can walk, knowing there are others who can't.

3. Work your way up to what you love and appreciate about yourself. Your gratitude can begin with the small stuff and build to the bigger stuff—you. However, if you feel like jumping right into the big stuff, then go ahead. Over time, you will find that you become so much more appreciative of everything. This, in turn, allows others to appreciate you. Since the world is a mirror, we change it by changing ourselves. Eventually, we will be able to focus on loving and appreciating ourselves, both on the list and off. This will help us to embody more fully who we are as spirit.

For example:

WHAT I AM GRATEFUL FOR...

I am grateful for the air I am breathing, I am grateful for my legs that carry me places, I am grateful for the trees and the sound of the birds, I am grateful for the home I live in and the garden outside my window blossoming with fresh vegetables waiting to be picked, I am grateful for my family, their health, and well-being, I am grateful for my puppy who makes me smile no matter what mood I am in, I am grateful for listening to my inner guidance, I am grateful for being spirit led, I am grateful for the wisdom that flows through me, I am grateful for my kind heart, I am grateful for taking the time to work on myself...

Your Gratitude List may begin with all the reasons why you are grateful, like your family, your job, the clean air, or the food on your table, but it needs to end with what you love and appreciate about yourself. This way you begin to value yourself more and more, eventually leading to self-love. There is nothing you cannot be, do, and have when you love yourself. This is not ego love. It is recognizing that your spirit is love. All the love that you have been seeking externally can be found in your connection to your spirit.

As you can see, your list will be unique to you. You may find that, as a daily practice, your list may see many recurring items in addition to changes. You can't repeat gratitude too often. It is a way to express your true nature while training the mind to habitually focus on appreciation. The more we appreciate life, the better we live it, as we recognize it for the gift that it is.

Let me tell you about a client who completely transformed her life within one year using these two transformational tools: the Let Go and Know List and the Gratitude List. Like many of us, self-criticism held her back from living the life she was meant to live. After learning these simple tools, she changed things dramatically by applying them in her life.

Struggling with beating herself up (sound familiar?), she made a commitment for a one-year period to put her focus on stopping this destructive behavior and forming a new one that would promote self-love and appreciation. She did not take this task lightly, nor did she give up when the fruits of her labor seemed fruitless. She consistently kept at it, completing her Let Go and Know List and the Gratitude List every day, despite the lack of obvious results. Toward the end of the year, things began to change in a big way. Her marriage improved, her business flourished, her friendships blossomed, her creativity expanded, her dreams began to bear fruit, and, most importantly, her contribution to the world was realized—the contribution that only she could make. My client stopped doubting her gifts and began giving them fully, leading to a life of purpose. This left my client in a place of utter amazement that one simple practice, done consistently over a period of time, could change her so much.

She woke up every morning and on a sheet of paper wrote down every fear, complaint, and negative thought about herself (or anyone else for that matter) and burned it. She, in essence, cleared the mind of any toxic thoughts. At first, there were many, but over time, fewer and fewer seemed to appear on the list. Immediately after doing this each day, she would fill her mind with what she wanted to focus her thoughts on—what she loved and appreciated about herself. She filled an entire journal page every day with compassionate, loving, and truthful words. The more she wrote them, the more truthful they became to her. She noticed that at first it was difficult to find things to appreciate about herself, so she would focus on what she was grateful for in general. This allowed her to raise her vibration enough to begin to even be able to see what was worth appreciating about herself. After a while, she could just dive right into what she loved about herself.

This practice changed the way she saw herself, and it changed the way she made choices. She was no longer holding herself back by doubt and self-criticism. She knew that what she had to offer was valuable and she gave it freely. This attracted others to her. As a result, she expanded her service in the world and was happier doing it.

If you really want to give your vision a chance to come to fruition, give this practice a try (I mean really do it consistently). It will change you for the better. Louise Hay says it well: "You have been criticizing yourself for years, and it hasn't worked. Try approving of yourself and see what happens."

CONSCIOUSLY CHANGING YOUR VIBRATION LEVEL

When we feel good, it is an indicator that we are vibrating at a higher vibration. We do not have to wait for something external to make us feel better; we can consciously choose our vibration now. We already know everything in creation is made up of energy of varying frequencies. Our emotions alert us to the vibration at which we are currently vibrating. Vibrations act as a magnet, so we will tend to draw to us vibrations of a similar frequency, those with which our vibrations resonate. When two vibrations are close enough in frequency, they create what is called a resonant field. This means that when one vibration meets another vibration, the two vibrations will slightly adjust themselves until they are vibrating together at an identical frequency.

This means that if you wake up in a "bad" mood and don't adjust your vibration, you will probably have a "bad" day, attracting situations that match your own negative vibration. However, if you raise your vibration, you will notice that you also attract matching positive vibrations throughout your day. The good news is that if you keep your vibration high, resulting in much more positive emotional states, you will naturally raise the vibration of those around you. This creates healing and harmony wherever you go. The reason this works is because, if two vibrations are close but not the same, the weaker vibrational field will tend to change its energy to match that of the higher vibrational field until it is vibrating at the same frequency. Conversely, if your vibration is too discordant with another much lower vibration, the person with the much lower vibration will have a tendency to move away from you like a repelling effect.

Have you ever gone to lunch with a friend and left feeling completely drained? When you arrived you were feeling good, but when you left, not so much. You matched the vibration of your friend without realizing it. It happens all the time by confusing compassion with sympathy and lowering our vibration in an effort to match our friends where they are instead of remaining at the vibration that is aligned for us. We have also had the opposite experience, where we went to visit someone when we weren't feeling so great and left feeling much better. Our vibration lifted to match theirs like a contagious smile. The important thing to realize is we do not need to be reactive to another's vibration—we just need to consciously change our own. When we do, we spread this vibration to others, bringing more healing and harmony into the world.

VIBRATION CHART		
COLOR	AUDITORY	FEELING
Gold	20,000 Hz – Infinity	Joy • Love • Awareness
Silver	15,000 – 20,000 Hz	Peace • Gratitude • Knowing
White	10,000 – 15,000 Hz	Passion • Compassion • Seeing
Purple	6,000 – 10,000 Hz	Happiness • Understanding
Blue	3,000 – 6,000 Hz	Hopeful • Accepting • Forgiving
Green	1,000 – 3,000 Hz	Neutral • Content • Allowing
Yellow	500 – 1,000 Hz	Proud • Discontent • Doubting
Orange	100 – 500 Hz	Frustrated • Impatient • Judging
Red	80 – 100 Hz	Angry • Disappointed • Accusing
Brown	40 – 80 Hz	Fear • Jealous • Blaming
Black	20 – 40 Hz	Hate • Shame • Condemning
Gray	1 – 20 Hz	Grief • Disconnect • Isolation

NOTE: The colors on the Vibration Chart will vary from individual to individual.

The Vibration Chart correlates color or vibration with emotional states and auditory frequencies. When we are feeling isolated and disconnected, we are very low on the vibrational scale. When we are feeling joy and love, we are very high on the vibrational scale. If you look at the corresponding colors, you will notice gray is associated with isolation and disconnection, whereas the color gold is associated with joy and love. This is what is naturally happening inside our energy field when we feel these feelings. The color of our energy field changes depending on how we are vibrating (remember the aura photos in chapter 2). Once we understand how this works, we can consciously change our vibration by changing the color of our Spirit Bubble. This Vibration Chart is a conceptual model, as the colors and auditory frequency ranges will be different for each person. What constitutes a high and low vibration for you is unique. Let your spirit guide you to the colors that are appropriate for you. Remember, everyone's path is different, so one color will resonate for you and another will resonate for someone else. When using this chart, the key is to be Centering, Clearing, and Connecting. In this way, you can be guided by your spirit to the color that is in alignment for you. When you notice you have dropped to a lower vibration, either by the way you feel or the color of your Spirit Bubble, you can change it by using this transformational tool.

I once ran through a stop sign—not on purpose, but because I wasn't paying attention and didn't see it, nor did I see the cop hiding around the corner. Apparently, many people ran this particular stop sign. As soon as I saw the police officer turn on his flashing lights, I panicked. I was certain I was going to get a ticket. I pulled over, and it seemed it took the officer a while to get out of the car. Instead of continuing to worry, I realized my bubble was a very low vibration (brown), so I changed the color to a soft blue. I filled my entire body and beyond with this soothing blue light until it extended five feet in all directions. I immediately felt peaceful and neutral to the situation. When the officer approached, I was already smiling. He asked me some questions. I answered them. He took out his pad and said, "Today is your lucky day; I am not going to give you a ticket." As you can imagine, I was happy about that, but not dependent on it to feel good. I know luck had nothing to do with it. If I hadn't changed the color of my

Spirit Bubble, I would have gotten that ticket.

What is your highest and best vibration? There is a color that represents it. By actively visualizing this color, you can change your vibration almost instantly. By using the next tool, you are going to find out how to do this so you can resonate at your best vibration whenever you choose.

TRANSFORMATIONAL TOOL #14:
THE COLOR OF YOUR SPIRIT BUBBLE (CHANGE YOUR VIBRATION)

1. Think of a time when you were feeling great—what I mean is, you were feeling connected to something greater than yourself. Imagine that experience; it can be absolutely any time, even way in your past. For example, maybe you are on top of a mountain soaking in the rays of the sun or you are in your favorite place in nature taking in the beauty and peace around you or you are with those you love the most, feeling your heart opening and expanding... You get the picture. These are moments from your life where you are thriving, connected, and full of love.

2. Now, feel the feelings you had in that moment, really sink into them. Spend at least two minutes with these positive feelings.

3. Allow a color to come to you directly from your spirit that represents this high vibrational state you are currently in. Do not judge the color, just know what it is and trust what you get.

4. Imagine this color within you and surrounding you now, five feet in all directions, 360 degrees, filling your Spirit Bubble. You are immersed in a bubble of this color. Become aware of how it feels to you. If you feel great, this is a color that allows you to vibrate higher. If it doesn't feel right, go back and do the process again. The example below shows a person in a blue Spirit Bubble. By imaging this color around them, they not only feel better and vibrate

higher, but they also deflect any negative or low vibrational energy from entering their bubble.

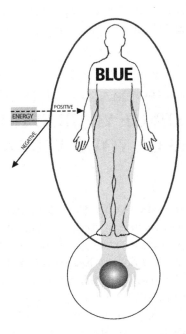

Life happens, and you can make the best of it by choosing the color of your Spirit Bubble; this allows you to vibrate at your best. This changes the world around you almost instantly. You can also use this tool by placing a bubble of colored light around your home and your car just by visualizing it. This tool will not only enhance your daily experiences, but is very handy to use in any stressful situation to clear the energy of stress and replace it with how you want to feel. You do this by simply changing the color of your Spirit Bubble, and you automatically change your personal vibration, bringing more harmony to those around you.

Don't leave your house without your Spirit Bubble. It allows you to resonate at a higher vibration, feel better, and attract in experiences that are also of a higher vibration. Life just keeps getting better and better the more you use this transformational tool.

HOMEPLAY

☐ Complete your list from Transformational Tool #11: Energy Drains to Energy Givers. Then pick three things from this transformational tool to focus on each day. Notice how you are developing new habits just by putting your awareness on what gives you energy. Over time, this compounds and you have more energy than you ever thought was possible, raising your vibration to new levels.

☐ When you find you are stuck and can't move beyond a situation from your past, applying Transformational Tool #12: Forgive for Good will begin to give you the freedom you seek.

☐ Every day for the next week, use Transformational Tool #13: Gratitude List with a Twist. Fill a page in your Gratitude Journal each day, paying particular attention to writing about what you love and appreciate about yourself. Observe your level of appreciation rising in conjunction with your vibration. Notice how many more people in your life begin, overtly, appreciating you.

☐ Each morning before you leave the house, apply Transformational Tool #14: The Color of Your Spirit Bubble. Consciously change the color of your Spirit Bubble to the color that makes you feel your highest and best. Notice how you feel. Later in the day, if you find that you are not happy, see what color your Spirit Bubble has become and change it back to where you want it to be. Feel great, no matter what is going on around you. Observe how this higher vibration draws to you many more positive experiences.

CHAPTER SIX

How to Unleash the Visionary in You

"Vision…It reaches beyond the thing that is, into the conception of what can be.
Imagination gives you the picture. Vision gives you the impulse
to make the picture your own."
- Robert Collier

When I was in my early twenties, I noticed that my best ideas came to me in two very unusual places: in the shower and when I was sleeping. In fact, I was in the shower when I looked down and saw the ball chain on the tub stopper and knew I needed to go to the hardware store and design a line of jewelry. This silly vision that I chose to act upon became my first line of jewelry and ended up becoming a million-dollar company. My vision continued to reveal itself in my dreams, where I would wake up and know the specifications of a product I was to design. Some of these became award-winning patented products. I would sleep with a pad next to my bed because I never knew when a new idea might come to me. I became curious about where the ideas were coming from and why it happened at such seemingly bizarre times. How could I access this experience when I wanted to? The answer came to me many years later, and it is one of the reasons I do the work I do today.

The answer is simple. The mind cannot give us our vision. Vision comes from our spirit. It appeared that the only two places in my life where my mind turned off was when I was sleeping or in the shower. This allowed the door to my spirit to open, where my vision began shining through. If all it takes for our vision to come through is getting our mind out of the way and connecting to our spirit, then this is where I want to be. I later learned that visionaries like Einstein understood this principle. As he put it, "The mind cannot solve the same problems it created." To facilitate his light-bulb moments (pun intended), Thomas Edison would go to sleep with a rock in his hand so he could be awakened with a new vision. As Edison would fall asleep, the rock in his hand would drop and wake him. It was here he found the sweet spot between sleeping and waking where his best ideas lived. He used this practice to get his mind out of the way and access his spirit. He had over 1,000 patents. Now, I don't believe it is necessary to sleep with a rock in your hand to access your vision; it is only a question of accessing your spirit. Your greatest vision is there. Edison said it well: "If we did all the things we were capable of, we would literally astound ourselves."

In this chapter, you will learn to uncover your greatness, to be the visionary you were always meant to be. Using the transformational tools I have previously shared with you, along with the new ones in this chapter, you will learn to access your vision. At this point in human history, now more than ever, the world needs your vision. It is incumbent upon each of us to be the visionaries that we are.

FROM THE INSIDE OUT

Where are the great resources of the world—you know, the wealth of the world, like oil, water, gas, diamonds, and gold? They all exist deep beneath the earth's surface. We are a reflection of the earth, and it is deep within us that our vision is. This is where we find our gold. But yet, this is often the last place we look. We are so certain that all the resources we need exist outside of ourselves that we spend most of our lives searching for them in the external world.

What if all the things we have ever dreamed of, like love, wealth, peace, joy, and freedom, existed within us? What if we were to learn that fulfillment and happiness were the very things we have been searching for outside ourselves, yet the truth is they have always been within us? There is an expression, "If God wanted to hide Himself from human beings, the best place would be inside of them because that is the last place they would look." It is inside of us where spirit lives. Accessing it is where we find our greatness. It is not in some of us, but in all of us.

WHY WE ARE ALL VISIONARIES

Why do some of us believe that we are less than the greatness that we are—that it is a stroke of luck that leaves a few of us with vision and most of us without? It is easy to look at Gandhi, Martin Luther King, Jr., Mother Teresa, and Leonardo da Vinci and acknowledge that they are all visionaries. We believe that they were just born that way, as some of us are, but most of us are not.

What if this is a false belief and we are actually all unrealized visionaries? Surely, people believed that the world was flat until a visionary challenged it. Let us begin with the belief that each and every person who walks this earth is a visionary. It is not so far-fetched to imagine that each and every human being has a great contribution to make to the world. And what would happen to the world if we believed in our vision enough to realize it? As a Spirit Coach, teacher, and fellow human being, I see every day in the work I do that each and every one of us has a special gift, which, when realized, is our vision. It is our spirit that leads us there. When we bury this gift, not only do we lose out, but so does the world.

When we are born, we are full of the possibility of greatness because we are already connected to spirit. What happens over time, in most cases, is this part of who we are is not acknowledged by our families, our communities, and, most importantly, ourselves; thus, our spirit becomes buried within us and remains only the possibility of greatness.

What if we could reclaim our greatness at any point and take it back from the hard knocks of life that leave us stuck in mere struggle for survival at worst and a comfortable mediocrity at best? The truth is, no one or nothing can ever take away our greatness because it is our spirit. It may become buried with layers of illusion that we have come to believe is us, but at any time we can drop the illusion and acknowledge our spirit. We can then access our own vision by being spirit led and becoming the visionaries we were meant to be.

What we do and what we do not do affects others equally. Most of us think that by not exhibiting our gifts, the world is no worse off than it already is. This is where we are wrong. Often, we hold back from contributing or from putting ourselves out there because we believe we are a work in progress. Once we are perfect, then, and only then, can we let ourselves out into the public spaces of our lives. The truth is, we will always be a work in progress and we will never be perfect. Many people have expressed on their deathbed that it is not what they did that they regret, but what they didn't do. It is incumbent upon each of us to take a risk, take that leap of faith, and take that first step.

I have been way too much of a perfectionist in my life. I have swallowed my words in fear that they would come out wrong. I have chosen not to do things for fear I wasn't good at them. I have said no to many things because I was afraid I would fail. All the risks we are unwilling to take limit our lives and limit our growth. It does not need to be like that anymore.

When we hold back because we believe we aren't good enough or we are afraid we will fail, the world loses. Our vision and our gifts are unique to us. If we don't allow ourselves to shine, others will not be illuminated by our glow.

WHERE TO BEGIN

We begin on the visionary path by choosing love. What is it that you love? What is the one thing you would do just for the sake of doing it? For me, it has always been teaching others. When I was six years old, I would pretend with my neighborhood friends that I was the teacher and they were my students. I loved helping my friends discover the joy in learning. This came absolutely naturally to me—no one told me to play this way.

What we love is what we play. We often did this as a child, and if we are spirit led, we are still doing it now. Joseph Campbell said, "Follow your bliss." He was not talking about ego gratification, but that deep love that is within us. No one can tell us what it is; we just know it. It is a resonance that comes from our spirit.

The next tool I am going to show you allows you to explore what makes your heart sing. If your heart is the window, your spirit is the door. Your heart can lead you to your spirit, and your spirit will open the door to your vision.

TRANSFORMATIONAL TOOL #15:
TOP 10 THINGS THAT MAKE YOUR HEART SING

1. Practice the five-minute meditation before you begin this process. It will allow the door to your spirit to open; you will receive more information this way.

2. Take out a sheet of paper or use the Playsheet provided. Then write down at least ten things that make your heart sing. These are the things you absolutely love, from the small things to the big ones. They do not need to have any logical reason why you love them. In fact, it is much better if they don't—then you know your mind is not involved in this process.

For example:

1. Reading a really good book

2. Writing poetry

3. Watching the sunrise

4. Listening to beautiful music

5. Dancing

6. Creative projects: cooking, watercolor, making jewelry

7. Spending time in nature

8. Helping someone in need

9. Connecting with good friends

10. Writing short articles with helpful tips

3. If you are having a hard time, remember some of the things you loved as a child and write them down. You can also close your eyes and place your hand on your heart. Take a few deep breaths, inhaling deeply into your heart. Then, ask yourself, What would make my heart sing? Remember to keep it simple. Your heart will lead you to what your spirit knows to be true.

TOP 10 THINGS THAT MAKE YOUR HEART SING PLAYSHEET	
1	
2	
3	
4	
5	

6	
7	
8	
9	
10	

Go to www.spiritcoachtraining.com/playsheet for a free downloadable PDF

Now that you have your list, I recommend doing what I call a Blind Reading. This is when you let your spirit guide you to something without your mind dictating what that something is. For example, after your morning meditation, without looking at your Top 10 List, ask your spirit to show you what number lights up on your list. If you get the number three, then pick up your list and see what your spirit chose. Make a point of doing that item today. This is a great way to integrate what you love into your daily life. Making time for what you love will lead you to your greatest vision.

FINDING YOUR VISION IN
UNLIKELY PLACES

Many years ago, I was leading a Vision Retreat. After a guided meditation, I asked the participants to draw their vision. One participant, Dabney, stood up and exclaimed very loudly, "I can't draw, and I don't want to do it." I merely suggested that if he was having this much resistance to drawing, it was exactly what he needed to do, explaining that, often when we move through our resistance, we find the very thing we have been looking for on the other side. Dabney decided to take a leap of faith and draw.

In the end, Dabney was quite pleased with his drawing. It was a beautiful landscape nestled in the woods on a fire trail with a fire lookout. It brought him a sense of peace, so he took it home and pinned it on his bulletin board where he saw it every day. Below is Dabney's drawing in black and white; it was originally drawn with colored crayons.

Several months later, Dabney was out of state visiting his partner's son, who insisted that they look at a piece of property that was for sale. They were in the woods driving down a fire trail when, all of a sudden, Dabney had a strange feeling like he had been here before. In that moment, he realized that he was smack in the middle of his drawing. Next thing he knew, he was looking at the fire lookout that he drew with crayons months earlier at the retreat. Dabney was so taken with this place that he bought the property, moved to Oregon, and is now, literally, living his vision. The following is a photo of the property Dabney bought.

Of course, I have had my own success with this technique, which is why I teach it. To put it kindly, drawing was never my best medium, so the idea of it made me, let's just say, avoid it entirely. However, when I was looking for a home and couldn't find it, I decided to draw it. I meditated and asked my spirit to show me the perfect home for my family. I paid attention to the feelings I felt about my visionary home; the colors that I used represented those feelings. Interestingly enough, I had drawn angels on one side of the house. After the drawing, I did find my dream home, and it looks a lot like my picture (at least to me). It even has an angel naturally impressed in the marble in my bathroom. When I saw this, I knew it was my spirit's vision realized.

TRANSFORMATIONAL TOOL #16:

DRAW YOUR VISION

1. Get a piece of paper and some crayons ready before you begin this process.

2. Practice The Three Cs for a minimum of five minutes. Centering, Clearing, and Connecting will give you access to your highest vision.

3. Then, as part of your meditation, imagine you are going to your highest and best life, five years in your future. Yes, time travel. Imagine getting into a golden elevator and go up. As you move to higher and higher floors, you feel less attached to your current reality. You will know when you arrive at five years into your future, as the doors will open.

4. Look around. What does it feel like, what are you doing, who are you with? Do not judge what you see, just take it in. Spend a few minutes there.

5. When you return back to present time, take your crayons and draw whatever it is you saw. It may not make sense. This is a good thing; it means your mind is out of the way.

6. Use colors you are drawn to, creating the symbols and images you observed in your vision. Do not judge, just allow.

7. Repeat this process several times to access more and more—this may be the path to accessing your greatest vision.

TRANSFORMATIONAL TOOL #17:
JOURNAL YOUR VISION

The process you completed using the previous tool can also be accomplished by journaling your vision.

1. Get a piece of paper and a pen before you begin or use the Playsheet provided.

2. Start with your five minutes of Centering, Clearing, and Connecting.

3. Then, as part of your meditation, imagine you are going to your highest and best life, five years in your future. Yes, time travel. Imagine getting into a golden elevator and going up. As you move to higher and higher floors, you feel less attached to your current reality. You will know when you arrive at five years in your future, as the doors will open.

4. Look around. What does it feel like, what are you doing, who are you with? Do not judge what you see, just take it in. Spend a few minutes there.

5. When you return back to present time, take your pen and paper and write down everything you experienced. Write it as if you are in present time, i.e., your vision is happening right now. Write down in words, in a stream of consciousness, what it is you observed in your vision. Journaling is a wonderful way to access your spirit, that is, to go beyond the mind. It can uncover hidden insights about your vision. Journaling is a way to express your spirit without being concerned with or judging the result.

6. Let your writing flow as the words come forth; never edit yourself or worry about spelling or grammar. Journaling is a place of freedom; there are no rules. Let whatever is on the surface come forth, and eventually a deeper understanding about yourself and your vision will emerge.

JOURNAL MY VISION PLAYSHEET

MY VISION

Write it as if you are in present time. Your VISION is happening right now.

_____

_____

_____

_____

_____

_____

_____

_____

_____

_____

_____

_____

_____

_____

_____

_____

_____

_____

_____

_____

_____

_____

Go to www.spiritcoachtraining.com/playsheet for a free downloadable PDF

This process may take some time, so be gentle with yourself. If your vision does not make sense at first, just be with it without judging it as good or bad. Ultimately, when you allow your spirit to lead you, you may not know the big picture; it is about trusting and taking one more step closer to your vision. If we did know the big picture, it would probably be too small for us to live.

By using these two transformational tools, you are asking spirit to guide you in accessing your greatest vision. You are not allowing the mind to dictate what it thinks is best for you. By reaching beyond the mind, you tap into something much greater and much more aligned with your spirit, who you really are.

VISIT YOUR FUTURE TO CREATE
YOUR BEST NOW

One of my clients had read Jack Canfield's book, *The Success Principles*. In the book, Jack talked about a party that he participated in that was five years in his future. Everyone at the party showed up as if they were living the life they wanted. Five years later, many of them, including Jack, were actualizing their vision. This inspired my client to bring Jack's idea to one of my Vision Retreats in the Canadian Rockies.

About forty of us were helicoptered in to a resort on top of a ten-thousand-foot mountain, where we explored what it meant to be a visionary. One night, we had a party, five years in the future. How did we do this? We time traveled. We picked a date five years from the current one and pretended it was today. Our vision of our highest and best life was being actualized in this moment, at the event. We were to show up at the party as if we were living this life.

To do this, to know how we would show up, we first had to discover who it is we wanted to be. We had to do this work first. We went deep into our self and asked our spirit. These qualities became who we would be when we showed up at the event.

This was one of the best parties I have ever been to because everyone was happy. You can guarantee that was on the top of everyone's list. What was amazing is that no one had to wait five years from now to be happy because everyone was doing it in the now. This was only one of many illuminating discoveries we made that evening. There is no need to wait for something external to make us happy; we can choose it, right now.

We also realized the importance of sharing our vision with each other. Every person stood in front of the group and described their vision. It was moving beyond the words that were spoken. Everyone in that room could feel the vibration and presence of each person's vision. The second discovery came when we realized the power of sharing: to really feel our vision and share them with others out loud brought us that much closer to them.

The amount of gratitude in the room was palpable. Everyone was in so much appreciation of each other, who they were being, and what they brought to life. Learning to appreciate the moment is another gift we learned that night.

Everyone created a Vision Board of their life, five years in the future, and we displayed each one for everyone to see. Writing down our vision, seeing the words and images that are a reflection of who we are and what we are creating is one of the keys to achieving that vision.

That night, each of us recognized that it had so little to do with what we wanted to be doing five years from now, but much more to do with who we were being. When we follow who we want to be, all the doing comes naturally from there. This is why Gandhi said, "Be the Change."

About four years after this event, I received an email from a client who had participated. He had just found what he had written atop that Canadian mountain and sent it to me. He was so blown away at how this so completely and accurately mirrored the life he is living now. *And he did it in four years, not five.*

There is no need to go to a mountaintop to see who you want to be. Apply the tools in this chapter, creating your own list of who you would like to be and what you would like to experience five years from now, two years from now, or even one year from now. Do not minimize the power of your spirit to create the life of your dreams. As Walt Disney said, "If you can dream it, you can do it." Don't forget, he created "the happiest place on earth." And so can you.

HOMEPLAY

☐ Complete your list from Transformational Tool #15: The Top 10 Things That Make Your Heart Sing. Each day, pick one thing from the list to integrate into your daily life. If you find you picked a big item, ask yourself what one small step you can take today toward achieving it. Notice how much happier you feel when you are doing the things that make your heart sing.

☐ Carve out some time for you, maybe on the weekend, to unleash your vision. Practice your five-minute meditation first and then visualize your spirit time traveling into your future. Whether it is two, three, or five years, be open to what you observe, even if it doesn't make sense. Then, draw or journal your vision (Transformational Tool #16: Draw Your Vision and Transformational Tool #17: Journal Your Vision).

☐ Don't forget that the other tools in this book that you have already learned will really help you in accessing, and then actualizing, your vision. We need to create a way for our vision to be part of our day-to-day experience. We can do this by applying the transformational tools in this book. This may mean setting a Daily Intention, spending more time being rather than doing, to achieve your vision with less effort. It may also mean using the Let Go and Know List when you get frustrated that your vision is not moving fast enough and applying the Gratitude List to keep your vibration high.

CHAPTER SEVEN

LET WHAT YOU SEEK FIND YOU

"The path of the co-creator is to be awakened spiritually within, which then turns into your own deeper life purpose, which then makes you want to reach out and touch others in a way that expresses self and really evolves our communities and our world. Certainly, we can't do that unless we activate ourselves first. That's why, for me, emergence is the shift from ego to essence."
- Barbara Marx Hubbard

The homeless man and mystic who told me that I wanted to help people but didn't know how set me on a course of finding my spirit. It was not too long after this profound encounter that I was sitting with John of God in Brazil, meditating and asking how I could serve others. I remember leaving the Casa, which is the center for miracle healing, with a feeling that I was filled with light; I felt very connected to my spirit. I sat in the garden and took out my journal. What proceeded to flow out onto the page seemed to me like very clear chapter titles for a book, *or so I thought.*

When I returned home to California, I began writing and could not stop for the course of the next year. It was pouring through me like a river of

Divine inspiration, though at the time I was not even sure what it was. It turned out to be the Spirit Coach Method. This system of transformational tools to be spirit led was the answer to the question, "How I can serve others?" Since this time, I have used this method with thousands of people in helping them to become spirit led.

When I simply committed to the path of being spirit led, what I was seeking found me. The method poured through me. The people who were looking for this information came to me. I didn't have to make any of it happen. It happened completely on its own. When we are spirit led, we no longer have to search. What we are seeking finds us. This does not mean we don't have to do anything. We do, but it is often not what we think we need to be doing. "Think" is the operative word. When we exit the vantage point of the mind, we can see where our spirit is directing us. The only thing that is required of us is to pay attention, listen, and follow spirit's guidance.

It is important to understand I am not in any way special. We all have a gift to give, and when we do, we actualize our service in the world. When we are spirit led, the gift is given and we, in turn, give it back. This is the miracle of being spirit led; we are meant to live in the age of miracles. You will know your own miracle when you experience it. It is waiting to be born within you.

BRING YOUR VISION TO FRUITION
USING CO-CREATION

Life happens, and we often don't make the time to listen to that small, subtle voice of spirit that can lead us to our greatest life experiences. This is why we need to apply tools to make sure it is woven into the very fabric of our everyday life. One of my favorite tools to make this happen is the Co-Creation To-Do List. Most of us have our daily to-do list, whether we keep it in our head or write it down. This is a similar list, but the intention behind it is very different.

You don't have to do it all yourself. One of the great things about being spirit led is you become a co-creator. Co-creation does things for you even quicker and better than you could ever imagine. Put all those to-dos floating around in your head, not to mention your vision that you need to make more time for, on the Co-Creation To-Do List. This is a way that you and Creator can work together to make it all happen. Yes, you and Creator can work together. Now that is a powerful team.

Each day, it is your job to determine which items on your Co-Creation To-Do List you absolutely, beyond a shadow of a doubt will do today. This means only what you will do, not what you plan to do or think you can do. It may only be one or two things, which is okay. Place those things on the "Me" side, and everything else, including your vision, goes on the "Creator" side. Your intention is that Creator will help you do the rest. This exercise requires discernment, trust, and faith. If you are feeling overwhelmed or just want to increase your capacity to co-create, this is the tool to use.

TRANSFORMATIONAL TOOL #18:
THE CO-CREATION TO-DO LIST

1. Get a sheet of paper or copy the Playsheet provided.

2. To create your list, make two columns. Label the first column "Creator" and the second "Me."

3. Everything that you need to do, want to do, and don't want to do—from picking up the dry-cleaning to writing that book—goes on the "Creator" side. Yes, you are giving it all to Creator.

4. On the "Me" side, write all the things you know you are going to complete today—*and nothing more.* Guess what? You get to check it off at the end of each day and go to sleep feeling complete, accomplished, and good about yourself. Isn't that a nice change of pace?

For example:

CO-CREATION TO-DO LIST PLAYSHEET	
CREATOR	ME
Call Thomas	Doctor's appointment
New website design	Pay Visa bill
Develop blog	Client call
Attract life partner	
Email Angela	
Register January workshop	
Write book proposal	
Buy a new desk	
Pick up dry-cleaning	

The "Creator" side eventually begins to get done as well, sometimes miraculously and other times practically by slowly moving one thing at a time to the "Me" side. Never underestimate the power of co-creation that is ultimately reinforced by this practice.

Recently, I put an elliptical machine on my "Creator" side, and a week later, someone at a party asked if I knew anyone who wanted a free elliptical machine. Thanks, Creator. Now I have time to work out, and I get to cross not one, but two things off my list!

CO-CREATION TO-DO LIST PLAYSHEET	
CREATOR(God)	ME
move	Journal / meditate / visualize
Heal shoulders	SAvers -
Release neg. energy	Exercise
Insight re: job - Shine	
Receive favor	
Receive $ suddenly	

Go to www.spiritcoachtraining.com/playsheet for a free downloadable PDF

As you use the Co-Creation To-Do List on a daily basis, you will begin to have time for the things that really matter to you. Your vision no longer takes a backseat, because now your spirit is driving the car.

A SPIRIT-LED DAY

I have given you eighteen transformational tools in this book. At this point, it may feel a little overwhelming. What do I use and when? How often would it benefit me to use a specific tool? I am going to show you what you could apply in an average day. Over time, you will see how much benefit the tools give you and you will use them more often. For now, it is about slowly integrating them into your life. I am going to show you what a spirit-led day might look like when you are beginning.

The first thing I suggest you do is your spiritual practice. How you start the day sets the precedent for the rest of your day. Remember The Three Cs? This is your five-minute meditation practice:

TRANSFORMATIONAL TOOL #3:

CENTERING—YOUR GROUNDING CORD (page 42)

TRANSFORMATIONAL TOOL #4:

CLEARING—YOUR SPIRIT BUBBLE (page 44)

TRANSFORMATIONAL TOOL #5:

CONNECTING—YOUR CONNECTION TO SPIRIT (page 47)

Throughout your day, you may want to use your Grounding Cord, especially when you become unfocused or less present. If you use your Grounding Cord consistently, you will notice you are much more aware and calm. You can also go through your day with your Spirit Bubble; this allows what is not aligned to be deflected and what is aligned to enter. This is especially helpful when your day includes meeting with people who you know tend to drain your energy.

After your five-minute spiritual practice, set your Daily Intention for the day. This is who you want to be today. Let your spirit guide you to the two or three qualities you can be today.

TRANSFORMATIONAL TOOL #6:

SET A DAILY INTENTION (page 60)

Write it down on a sticky note, electronic device, or on the top of the Co-Creation To-Do List and keep it in the forefront of your awareness all day.

Before jumping into your day, you can use the Co-Creation To-Do List to see what the aligned to-do items are for you today. Let yourself be a co-creator and you will accomplish more with less effort.

TRANSFORMATIONAL TOOL #18:

CO-CREATION TO-DO LIST (page 127)

When you need to increase your discernment, use Transformational Tool #10: Replacing "I Should" with "I Choose" to see if an action you would like to take is aligned for you. If it is, choose it by bringing 100 percent of your energy to whatever it is you are choosing to do today.

TRANSFORMATIONAL TOOL #10:

REPLACING "I SHOULD" WITH "I CHOOSE" (page 81)

If you find during the day that your energy is low, you can do a quick Gratitude List to raise your vibration.

TRANSFORMATIONAL TOOL #13:

GRATITUDE LIST WITH A TWIST (page 99)

When frustration, anger, or judgment creep in, it may be time for a Let Go and Know List. If you don't have any paper, a pen, or a way to burn it, you can do a Rose-Release Meditation instead to release the thoughts and feelings that are not serving you.

TRANSFORMATIONAL TOOL #2:

THE LET GO AND KNOW LIST (page 27)

TRANSFORMATIONAL TOOL #9:

ROSE-RELEASE MEDITATION (page 77)

Finally, make time for your vision today. Pick one thing off your list of the Top 10 Things That Make Your Heart Sing and do it today.

TRANSFORMATIONAL TOOL #15:

TOP 10 THINGS THAT MAKE YOUR HEART SING (page 113)

These transformational tools may seem like a lot to do at first. Start wherever you are comfortable and build from there. You will find that the more you use these tools, the more time and energy you create. So just get started.

I am providing you with a Transformational Tool Checklist. It is a reminder of all the Spirit Coach Method tools you have read about in this book. One way I like to use this list is by doing a Blind Reading. After I practice The Three Cs, I see a number between one and eighteen light up. That's the number of the tool I need to use today. I let my spirit direct me to the tool that will be most beneficial for me; my spirit knows exactly what I need.

TRANSFORMATIONAL TOOL
CHECKLIST

Use this list to review what you have learned as well as how to integrate each tool into your daily life in deeper ways. You now have the tools for transformation. This knowledge only becomes wisdom when you apply it.

When you apply the tools for transformation, *all things are possible.*

As you embark on your own journey of actualizing your vision in the world and serving others, you will want to apply the tools of transformation to get you there.

TRANSFORMATIONAL TOOLS AND INFINITE BENEFITS

1. **Quiet Your Mind**

   Stops the mind from spinning, creates more peace, helps you to be present, supports you in moving into a calm and relaxed state

2. **The Let Go and Know List**

   A constructive way to release negative thoughts and feelings, cultivates awareness of your patterns, helps you forgive yourself and others

3. **Centering—Your Grounding Cord (part of The Three Cs)**

   Brings you out of the past or future into the present, centers you, connects you to something greater, creates a feeling of security and strength in spirit, mind, and body

4. **Clearing—Your Spirit Bubble (part of The Three Cs)**

   Raises your vibration, making you feel better, deflects non-aligned energy, allows you to attract higher vibrations

5. **Connecting—Connection to Spirit (part of The Three Cs)**

   Clears out limiting beliefs and false self and non-aligned energies, allows you to know your self in deeper ways, heals the spirit, mind, and body, creates inner peace and inner knowing, builds your intuition

---

6. **Set Daily Intention**

   Allows you to access the power of intention, create with less effort, increase focus and speed up results, allows you to Be

7. **Create "Be Time"**

   Allows you to know your self as spirit, teaches you to unplug, renews, cultivates creativity

8. **How to Discover Your Integrity Holes and Repair Them**

   Gets you in integrity with yourself, helps you discover your truth, allows you to manifest your vision

9. **Rose-Release Mediation**

   An energetic Let Go and Know List when you don't have a paper and pen, helping you to quickly release negative energy in the moment

10. **Replace "I Should" with "I Choose"**

    A discernment tool that helps you discover your aligned choices, not letting the "shoulds" run your life, empowering your choices

11. **Turn Energy Drains to Energy Givers**

    Eliminates energy losses, gives you more energy

12. **Forgive for Good**

    Allows you to forgive yourself and others, frees you from the past, creates better choices in the present, raises your vibration significantly, helps you learn from your mistakes

13. Gratitude List with a Twist

Allows you to raise your vibration, brings a more aware and positive perception to your life, increases self-love

14. The Color of Your Spirit Bubble

Allows you to maintain your highest and best vibration, empowers you to feel your best no matter who you are with or what you are doing

15. Top 10 Things That Make Your Heart Sing

Brings more joy into your daily life, helps you discover your authentic self, true vision, and contribution

16. Draw Your Vision

Gives you access to your greatest vision from your spirit's perspective through the medium of drawing

17. Journal Your Vision

Gives you access to your greatest vision from your spirit's perspective through the medium of writing

18. The Co-Creation To-Do List

Allows you to discern what is aligned action each day, reinforces your ability to co-create, resulting in more ease and less effort

These eighteen transformational tools are a sampling of what is available through the Spirit Coach Method. If you apply these tools in your own life, you will see significant changes in yourself and this will directly impact your experience. This does not happen by reading about them, you must apply the tools. Remember, you have nothing to lose, only to gain by practicing this method that many before you have used with great success. One of my clients describes it like this: "It is a system that helps people find their light inside, and then with the help of Divine energy, that light begins to shine brighter and brighter."

THE CONTRIBUTION YOU ARE
HERE TO MAKE

During the same visit to see John of God, where I received what was the beginning of the Spirit Coach Method, I also received an important lesson about the transformation process itself. As I approached the house I was renting for my stay there, it seemed to be covered with little black bugs that I must say made my skin crawl. When I went inside this small house, I saw hovering in the middle of the kitchen a giant blue butterfly. It seemed to be welcoming me home. In that moment, I realized those little black bugs I had been afraid of were actually caterpillars on their way to becoming extraordinarily beautiful butterflies. This was a metaphor for my own spiritual growth process, one that we all eventually go through. Often, we look at ourselves in the transformation process and we see only what we don't like instead of realizing we are in the process of transforming into the beautiful beings that we are—the result of which is revealing our unique beauty to the world.

A few days later, I was sitting in the orientation. A woman was seated directly in front of me, and I noticed there was a butterfly on her arm. It was a curious sight, as the orientation lasted about two hours and the butterfly did not leave her arm the entire time. When we were leaving, I asked her about it. She told me this butterfly had landed there a few hours ago and hadn't moved since. Then she explained the butterfly had landed on the same place where she has cancer. She had come to John of God to heal it. She and I both knew that it was already being healed.

Ever since those experiences, I have seen butterflies as a symbol of God. Whenever I see them, I say, "Hello, God." It is a reminder for me of the transformation we are all making to spirit, to our Divine selves. When we allow ourselves to make this shift to spirit, despite being uncomfortable and afraid, we emerge gloriously transformed, radiating more of our light into the world.

When it feels hard to move forward on our Divine path, one question that has helped me through is, "How can I serve?" When I understand that my personal transformation serves others, it inspires me to take my next step.

Through my work as a Spirit Coach, I have found that we all have a contribution to make and our spirit can lead us there. When we become spirit led, we not only reach a deep level of fulfillment because we are pursuing our calling, but we also serve others. Time and time again, I have seen that service becomes paramount when we are spirit led. This is why becoming spirit led changes the world, one person following spirit at a time.

Although people come to me for many different reasons, every single one ends up making a significant impact on their families, communities, and the larger world. Tim is a great example of this; he is a very successful businessman who decided something was missing in his life. When he came to me, he had a deep longing to connect to something greater. Everyone that knew him would say he was already great. He was, after all, at the top of his field, respected by thousands, and sought after as a role model. He, however, knew, there was a greater vision for himself to attain. As he began coaching with me, he found the voice of his spirit. It began to lead him to his contribution in the world. Unbeknownst to him, his spirit directed him toward a great passion for teaching children about peace. It was buried within him until his spirit revealed it. Of course, it was always there.

When he discovered that he wanted to educate children, he slowly began to work within his community to get peace education into the school system. He created gardens, where the children would learn to grow things and respect each other and the value of life itself. His vision grew as his connection to his spirit did. He did not initially know how to actualize his vision, but spirit led him to all the right people and places. Eventually, he created an entire city that is a community that prioritizes children. In fact, when you drive into his town, it says, right next to the name of the town and the population, "This is a child-honoring community." This has become a model for other cities and towns. His vision is his contribution to the world, and his spirit led him there.

Being spirit led changes the world, one person, one community, one city...at a time. When we are connected to our spirit, we know who we really are and what matters to us. From here, our vision begins to unfold. I have never met a visionary who does not serve others. A natural extension of being spirit led is to give. When we give is when we really begin to receive. It has been my experience that, in serving others, I am served.

Let me tell you about another client who truly serves others and, as a result, is fulfilled because she knows she is following her spirit's path.

Lisa owns her own business and is very active in her community. She has many friends and a loving family, but she still felt a void in her life. She found the work she was doing did not feed her spirit, and it left her wondering that there must be something more that she could experience from life. When she began working with me, her spirit led her down a path that was not at all expected.

During a meditation, she had a memory of her childhood. Lisa had been born with a cleft palate, and as a child, it was difficult for her to speak. Her family was poor, and they could not afford corrective surgery. It was not until Lisa was an adult with resources of her own that she was able to receive the surgery she needed. As you can imagine, this was a part of Lisa's life that she just wanted to forget, but for some reason, decades later, it came welling back up in her meditations.

It has been said, "It is in our wounding that we find our greatest gift." Lisa realized through the guidance of her spirit that she was being called to help children who were born with cleft palates get the surgeries they needed, even when their families couldn't afford it. Lisa's spirit guided her to become involved with an organization that did just that.

She began raising money for this cause and then, later, traveled to third world countries to help children get the surgery they needed, free of any cost to them. As of today, she has impacted the lives of over 800 children and their families, and she has impacted her own life by giving it great meaning. There is nothing that brings Lisa more fulfillment than helping a child smile again. Lisa is living her calling, and it is her spirit that led her there.

Imagine waking up each day inspired. This is what happens when you are spirit led; you become inspired. From here, there are no limits to what you can experience in your life. Ultimately, you will find that your spirit's path will lead you to the contribution you are here to make. There is nothing more fulfilling than knowing your unique contribution and living a life that revolves around it. I asked my grandfather, who lived to the ripe old age of ninety-two, what made his life extraordinary. He told me it was the contribution he made to others' lives. I have learned over the years of working with countless individuals that, when we are spirit led, our natural progression is to serve. With this comes such a deep level of peace, joy, and purpose in knowing we are contributing to the greater good. Your spirit knows what your contribution is. The tools in this book will help you get there. Now, all you have to do is apply them. I encourage you to let your inner vision blossom. You have a great contribution to make, and your spirit will lead you there. When you arrive, you'll experience a life more meaningful, content, and full of wonder than you ever imagined. This is the way we are all meant to live our lives—if we only stop letting life lead us and become spirit led instead.

ACKNOWLEDGMENTS

*L*et me just say I have a deep gratitude for those of you who picked up this book and don't really know why. You are trusting spirit to lead you to your highest and best life path. Thank you for trusting.

I would like to acknowledge the Foundation for Spiritual Development, where I received over a decade of training. I continue to learn, teach, and help build this non-profit organization dedicated to educating people to know themselves as spirit.

Thank you to my clients, past and present, who inspire me every day to create new tools for their transformation. Every time a client successfully uses a tool to transform themselves, I am honored to be a witness to their commitment and courage to pursue a spirit-led life. They have made me a better coach, trainer, and facilitator, and I have learned a great deal from them.

There are too many to personally list here, but I would like to thank the countless spiritual teachers I have studied with who pointed me to the truth within.

I would also like to thank the people who have chosen to become Certified Spirit Coaches and spread this transformational work throughout the globe. Your presence makes the world a better place.

I would like to thank the people who contributed to bringing this book to fruition: Debbie Gisonni, Barbara Filly, Stephanie Marohn, John Otto, Ronnie Sharpe, Amrito Cross, Lori A. Cheung, Patti McKenna, Alicia Dunams, Zoe Lonergan, Clint Willitt, and Stacey Lapuk.

I am truly grateful for my fellow teachers at the Foundation for Spiritual Development who call me on my "stuff" that I am unwilling or unable to see so that I can grow and serve others better: Dana Duryea, Eric Otto, Plamen Tanev, Susie Laurenson-Shipley, Lisa Kay, Kate Weigel, Walker Whelan, Sandy Pires, Rene Jenkins, Priscilla Curry, Kim Olson, Jill Jacobs, Elana O'Loskey, Chuck Collingwood, and Clint Willett.

I would like to thank my husband, Dana, for always supporting me in following my highest path and for teaching me and inspiring me to love more deeply every day.

Last, but certainly not least, I would like to thank Creator and my guides for your clear and direct guidance.

ABOUT THE AUTHOR

Jenai Lane today understands the difference between co-creating from a spirit perspective and creating from an ego perspective. She has allowed herself to follow her guidance and intuition, coming full circle, as she now lives her life knowing her purpose in this incarnation. Through her evolution on her spiritual path, she has studied with many enlightened teachers, trained in many intuitive and healing arts, and has experienced her own miracles, coming to the place of directing others on the path through Spirit Coaching.

Jenai began bringing spirituality into business by founding Zeal Company in 2000. It innovatively brought together life purpose, business creation, and spiritual development in a coaching forum. She inspired the hearts and souls of entrepreneurs across the country, assisting them in bringing their highest visions to the world. She is currently the Founder and President of Spirit Coach Training, where her Spirit Coach Methodology has been used for ten years with clients one on one, in retreat settings, and to train master coaches. Jenai is a principal teacher at the Foundation for Spiritual Development, a non-profit organization dedicated to educating people on how to experience themselves as spirit.

Jenai has a comprehensive understanding of the business world as a former Woman Entrepreneur of the Year. At the age of twenty-four, Jenai started her first award-winning company, Respect, Inc., and became an inventor of many patented and trademarked products. As a result, she appeared in media worldwide, from *The New York Times* to appearing on The Rosie O'Donnell Show. Jenai has been the recipient of numerous awards, notably the National Association of Women Business Owners (NAWBO) Woman Entrepreneur of the Year, and the Small Business Association's (SBA) Young Entrepreneur of the Year. She is featured in an array of books showcasing women and business.

Jenai currently lives in California with her husband, Dana, and their dog, Joy, where she coaches, writes, and co-creates her vision. She listens to her guidance and lives her life in service and gratitude for the people, beauty, and enriching experiences in her life.

IF THIS RESONATES WITH YOU, YOU MAY WANT MORE

*P*lease contact Spirit Coach Training for more information about our one-on-one coaching with a Certified Master Spirit Coach. This is a rare opportunity to turn an ordinary life into an extraordinary life. There is no limit to what you can co-create through this method. When you have the tools for transformation, all things are possible.

The Spirit Coach Method allows you to shift in a supportive and safe environment. You move at your own pace, learning to access Source directly where there is no longer a need for a teacher outside of yourself. You carry the seeds of all your desires. By going within, you can create that which you seek. As you become aligned with your spirit, you become the perfect expression of you, living your highest vision in the world.

Spirit Coach Training
369-B Third Street #428
San Rafael, California 94901-3581

Web: www.spiritcoachtraining.com
Email: coach@spiritcoachtraining.com

Awaken your Divine potential. Co-create your best life.

Made in the USA
Coppell, TX
27 May 2020

26556438R00085